THE MONK, THE TRUNK, AND THE JUNK

HOW PRE-DEATH CLEANING CAN BECOME PRO-LIFE GIVING

ALAN D. HARRIS

ECKHART & MAY
An imprint of The Apocryphile Press
PO Box 255
Hannacroix, NY 12087

Copyright © 2023 by Alan D. Harris
ISBN 978-1-958061-30-5 / paperback
ISBN 978-1-958061-31-2 / ebook

All rights reserved. No part of this book may be reproduced, stored in a retrieval system, or transmitted in any form or by any means—electronic, mechanical, photocopy, recording, or otherwise—without written permission of the author and publisher, except for brief quotations in printed or online reviews.

CONTENTS

Foreword Harold Ivan Smith, DMIN, FT	vii
Introduction	ix

PART ONE
WAKING UP

1. The Drive	3
2. The Day of Self-awareness and Looking Back	11
3. The Next Morning; the Journal Begins	21
Journaling Guide for Part I: Waking Up	27

PART TWO
FACING UP

4. The "Whys" and the "Whats" of Collecting and Keeping	31
5. The Rewards of Obtaining, Collecting, Accumulating, and Holding on to Things	41
6. Change = Loss = Grief	45
7. The Work	51
8. Getting Help	63
Journaling Guide for Part II: Facing Up	71

PART THREE
STEPPING UP

9. Self Care of Body, Mind, and Soul	77
10. The Path of Healing and Growth	86
11. Simplicity	92
Journaling Guide for Part III: Stepping Up	99

PART FOUR
LIGHTENING UP

12. Growth Through Letting Go 105
13. The Seventeenth day; Closing the Journal 114

Epilogue 117
Journaling guide for Part IV: Lightening Up 125
Journaling Guide for the Epilogue 127

APPENDICES

Rob's Rule 131
Robert Michael Shaw's "Rule of Life" 133
Rob's Rule Addendum: Simplicity &
Stewardship 137
Creating Your Own Rule of Life 141

Notes 143
Acknowledgments 149
About the Author 153

*This book is dedicated to my spouse Tracy,
my parents, our families, my colleagues, my clients,
and all those weighed down by their grief and their possessions.*

FOREWORD
HAROLD IVAN SMITH, DMIN, FT

I had no idea when Alan and I first began talking about this book that, in time, his insights would motivate me to not just read the final manuscript but to take his guidances and put them into concrete action. And to ask God's help to put good intentions into practice.

In our accumulation-frantic society, we have changed stuff from a noun to a verb, an action verb. We subconsciously conjugate the word "stuff." I stuff, you stuff, we stuff.... we all stuff. Because, truth be told, if we "all stuff" then I don't feel so bad about how much space in my life my stuff takes up. Or will soon take up.

Alan's *Monk* is important because we all have drawers, closets, plastic bins, storage sheds, and storage units, that are visible, at least to us. But what about the invisible spaces and places we store our stuff? Reading this book may annoy you. *Monk* might end up in your collection of "unread" books, riding in *your* trunk waiting for the next donation stop at a thrift store.

Alan asked me to do something more than read words on a page. He asked me to do something about my stuff, my clutter, my junk. Now. Put down this book and "Get at it!"

The temptation, is to say, well, rather than spending time reading this book, why don't I spent the time more productively by sorting, tossing, donating. Or re-storing my stuff, rather than restoring my soul.

Someone you know needs to read this book. I certainly needed to.

If only Alan's two questions could be tattooed on the inside of our eyelids, so that every time we blink we would see them: *What is all this stuff? Why am I carting all this around?* Or worse, *Why* am I storing it—or *paying* to store it?

Harold Ivan Smith, DMIN, FT

INTRODUCTION

This is a book about a man who goes through three different "wake-up calls" from childhood to later adulthood, who begins to explore life through its gains and losses, and who recognizes the spiritual growth possible in the "second half of life." Our story begins with Rob Shaw, an Associate of the Order of Saint Romanus, who after experiencing a tire blowout on his way to the monastery for a retreat, discovers that he can't get to the spare tire in the trunk because of all the junk crammed into it. He realizes the need to finally deal with the junk and the excess in his life, and begins both the inner and the outer work of that journey. Rob extends his brief silent retreat at the monastery in order to deeply explore his growth —and subsequently ours—through a lens of life transitions, grief, and possessions. From his experience—and through his journal—we witness the forward movement into mindfulness, simplicity, transformation, and transcendence.

The simple message in Rob's story is about acknowledging and unpacking the "junk" in one's life, while finding, keeping, and appreciating the "jewels." It is about recognizing who and what is important to us. As "pre-death cleaning," it is about making room for the essential by eliminating much of the clutter in our lives, not only for us but for those who follow us. Finally, it is a book on reflections and insights about collecting and collections: how we get started, and why we continue; how we use things for enjoyment, remembering, and healing, and yet how at times we become overwhelmed and burdened with these possessions. The purpose of this book is to cast light and offer help and hope on how we can grow—not only through dealing with our possessions and reducing clutter—but also through our recollecting and remembering through our grieving and giving. Following each section of the book there are journal questions that can be useful for the reader's reflection, hopefully serving as encouragement for your future work as you separate the jewels from the junk in your life.

In this story you will follow along with Rob on his trip to Saint Cecilia's monastery and what he sees as his third wakeup call along the way. You will benefit from the lessons of his three-day retreat—which expanded to seventeen days—as he shares his journal on "stuff" and possessions, and how they can either drag us down or lift us up through meaningful connections to our past, our loved ones, and our core values. Through his journal you will hopefully see what he sees, feel something of what he feels, and then be able to compare these insights to your own life's journey. At the end of the book, you can join him again a year later in the epilogue to read his "Rule of Life" that might perhaps serve as a template for developing your own personal rule.

With resilience, faith, and some freshly gained insights, Rob was able to rediscover new life with both an openness and a universalizing love in both his life and his spiritual care offerings to others.

So, join me, if you will, as we accompany Rob, as his retreat becomes a deep dive into people, possessions, and purpose, with a focus on the needs and values of belonging, connection, and meaning. Perhaps in some way you too will come away enlightened—with a lighter load yourself—toward repurposing and rededicating your life. Through this journey you too can discover for yourself the pro-life enhancing benefits of pre-death cleaning.

Alan D. Harris, DTh
www.worklifesoul.com

PART ONE
WAKING UP

CHAPTER 1
THE DRIVE

*"Sometimes you find yourself in the middle of nowhere,
and sometimes in the middle of nowhere you find yourself."*
—Stacy Westfall

*"Still, round the corner,
there may wait a new road or a secret gate."*
—J. R. R. Tolkien

Robert Michael Shaw was making the two-hour drive to Mount St. Cecilia's, a Benedictine monastery in Eastern Kansas, not far from the spot on the Missouri River where Lewis and Clark had docked and replenished their supplies almost 200 years before. Rob had begun making retreats at the monastery's tranquil setting several years ago after his studies in spiritual direction. He loved connecting with St. Cecilia's spiritual formation program, and had always enjoyed these times of retreat at "the motherhouse" to refocus.

While not speeding excessively, he was driving a bit more aggressively than usual due to his late start from home. Although it was typically more peaceful to head out a little early, this was not one of those times. Unfortunately, Rob always saw himself as contemplative, yet also punctual.

> *"Because the greatest part of a road trip isn't arriving at your destination. It's all the wild stuff that happens along the way."*
> —Emma Chase

About 12 miles after traveling through Schott's Township, Rob's car began to weave a bit, somewhat squirrelly he thought, before a loud "bang" interrupted this relatively peaceful—although spirited—drive to the monastery. Rob quickly grabbed the steering wheel with both hands as he put on the brakes, slowed down, and hobbled safely to the narrow shoulder on the two-lane road. Rob quickly gave thanks for being able to pull off the highway without injury or accident, then took a deep breath and turned on his hazard flashers. After checking to see that there was no other traffic approaching, he braced himself and got out of the car. *This might be bad, but it truly could have been much worse,* he thought to himself.

After getting out of the car, Rob saw that the driver's-side rear tire had blown. In the short period of time prior to pulling off the road, the tire had shredded and was obviously shot. *I've got a spare,* he realized, and decided that the best thing to do was to see if he could get someone from his insurance company's roadside assistance program to come out and replace the old tire with the spare. In the past, this was something he might have done himself, but he was now in his mid-60s, and it would be dangerous to do this work on such a narrow shoulder with a drop off just to his right. Yes, it would be best to call someone who might be a little more proficient at this type of work.

With a charged cell phone, and still within range of a cell tower, reaching and scheduling roadside assistance was easy. With about 45 minutes before the truck would arrive, Rob began the task of finding the small space-conserving spare in the trunk of his two-door coupe. Much to his dismay, it was easier said than done.

It became abundantly clear upon opening the trunk that his earlier resolutions to clean it out had been ignored. Rob had recently finished reading a book about making and keeping good habits, but obviously, having a clean and organized trunk had not been an important enough goal. And yes, the trunk was absolutely and completely full.

What is all this stuff? Why am I carting all this around? he thought, almost panicking when he realized the amount of work that lay ahead. The backseat was already spoken for by his travel bags and several weeks' worth of paperwork that he hadn't bothered to take back to his office. With about 30 minutes before roadside assistance was expected to arrive, Rob realized he had to figure out how to make the spare tire accessible. There was so much stuff in the trunk that the only thing he could do was to pull it all out and pile it behind the car. He dug out one partially filled box, thankful to have someplace to put the smaller items, and he began to stack the larger ones a few feet behind the car's rear bumper. Here is what he found: Bags of papers to recycle and shred. A dozen or so books to donate at the next book collection. Plastic water bottles to take to the recycling center and aluminum cans to drop off at the local VFW. A set of jumper cables and a half-filled jug of windshield fluid. He dug deeper as he began to sort and remove this unintentional collection from the trunk while finding the best way to stack it safely by the car. He found several folders of work papers and handouts from some groups he had led over the past three years. Then there were these: A smashed box of tissues, a spray bottle of windshield ice melt, and a blanket. The tissues could be helpful should his desperation turn to tears, but what use did he have for a blanket and ice melt in August? Making his way through the levels of stuff and into the depths of the trunk, he had to sort, push aside, and try to collect, in a couple of grocery bags, an assortment of trash—empty plastic cups, straws, food wrappers—along with a bag of clothes to donate to the local transitional housing center. *How did I let this get this bad?* he mused, as he finally reached the carpet that covered the spare tire compartment just as roadside assistance pulled up behind him with flashers on.

As he thanked the driver for coming out in his time of need, Rob found himself apologizing for the state of his trunk and its contents, now assembled in a couple of somewhat more or less organized stacks next to the car. *Why am I apologizing for this? Isn't it normal to have a collection of stuff like this in one's own car?* he thought. But then he caught himself in his rationalization just about the time that a stiff and sudden Eastern Kansas wind gust swept in, lifting, opening, and promptly dispersing through the air a large manila file folder full of assorted papers. It was as if they were immediately being called to some location other than where he had placed them. Frantic, Rob jumped into action. He tried to catch and recover the airborne papers that were soon scattered across the surrounding roadside drop off and the valley just beyond the shoulder. *How convenient,* he thought, watching them float into a nearby algae-covered pond, slowly drifting toward its center.

> *"When you go on a road trip, the trip itself becomes part of the story."* —Steve Rushin

Feeling stupid, and even helpless, for having files like these in his car trunk, he realized the futility of going after them. *Thank God these weren't from the bag of stuff to take to a future shredding event at the bank ... or were they?* No, he finally assured himself, they were just old handouts, notes from lectures, copies of meeting agendas, and other even less significant recyclable papers. He breathed a small sigh of relief before composing himself and accepted that what just flew away would be recycling itself, and one less thing for him to do. He returned his attention to the work the tow truck driver had just begun by jacking up the car after removing the spare from the now-empty trunk. In a matter of moments, the shredded tire was replaced with the spare.

After being assured that his insurance would pick up the tab, Rob thanked the driver as he signed the paperwork and offered another humble apology for the state of his trunk. He promised to get a new tire when he could over the next few days. Rob now started the work of repopulating his trunk with all that had come out of it, except for the long-lost papers that were now becoming one with the pond. Shaking his head, Rob got back into the car. With a deep sigh, he wondered if he should take the time to reflect on all this during the thirty minutes he had left in his trip to the monastery. *No*, he thought, *I'd better pay attention to getting there in a reasonable time, especially now that I'm driving on a tire that shouldn't be driven faster than 45 miles per hour. I'll find some time later to think about this.*

> "A certain monk went to Abbot Moses in Scete and asked him for a good word. And the elder said to him: Go, sit in your cell, and your cell will teach you everything." —Anonymous

Rob arrived a little later than he wanted, but evening prayer had yet to start. The community lived by the Rule of Benedict which structured not just the individuals' lives and routines, but the entire community's as well. While hoping to attend prayer, he thought it best to get his room key from the retreatant desk at the Sophia Center and make his first retreat tonight straight to his room. The little that he had reflected on since the road incident made him all too painfully aware that he had a lot to learn. He recalled the saying, "Go to your cell, and your cell will teach you everything." How many times had he read this, he wondered. The words were attributed to one of the early abbas and ammas, titles given the ascetic spiritual Desert Fathers and Mothers of the third and fourth centuries CE in Egypt, Persia, Palestine, and Arabia. While not seeing himself as having much in common with these predecessors of the monastic movement, he did see the point that some degree of isolation—time spent alone amid simple surroundings, separate from the world, with time for deep thought, contemplation, and prayer—was all one needed to deepen spiritually. Perhaps, he thought, this could help him in a lot of other ways. Rob's stress levels, work and church relationships, marriage, and certainly his organizational skills (or lack thereof) could stand for some improvement.

> "The first step toward change is awareness. The second step is acceptance." —Nathaniel Branden

Rob's "cell" was a clean, simple room with a shared bath. A twin bed, a small desk with a straight-back wooden chair and a lamp, a rocking chair, and a closet comprised the plain and simple furnishings. On one wall was a hand-made pottery cross. A window looked out over the fields and the spot where the old oak tree used to be. He sighed a breath of relief and felt right at home.

After putting his few things away, Rob checked the weekly calendar of the monastery that included the schedule for the daily hours. The "hours" are the times set aside for prayer, practiced by monastics and religious communities for over 1,500 years since the founding of the modern monastery by Saint Benedict of Nursia. St. Benedict had recognized the need for structure and support for the early monastics, with communal living and a daily rule to live by.

While envisioning this as a personal and mostly silent retreat, Rob was still open to the idea of having some worship and fellowship time with the community. In addition, he also wanted to take some spiritual direction with one of his favorite directors, either Sister Evelyn or Sister Margaret. While the other Benedictine monastery a few miles away was established as a community of monks and brothers, Saint Cecilia's was founded in the 1800s as a convent[1] for nuns and had grown to include a women's college and later the Sophia Center, the home of their program in spiritual formation. Father Jay, an Episcopal priest to whom Rob had been introduced by a deacon at church, was the one who had recommended the Sophia Center. For Rob, this became the place of his midlife spiritual awakening and formation. This is where he had first voiced "… all my springs of joy are in you," adapted from the 87th Psalm, to boldly proclaim to himself and the world that "all that is good that comes from me comes through this place."[2] Sophia, the feminine personification of wisdom, was an especially fitting and appropriate name for this special place, with its incredibly welcoming, kind, caring, and gifted community.

Rob suddenly remembered that he hadn't yet phoned home. He found he was unable to connect with a cell tower from his room, so he went outside and faced all four directions until he had enough reception to make a call. Rachel answered on the first ring. Rob apologized for the lateness of his call, letting her know that he got there safely and was just getting settled in. She expressed her relief, and glad to know he was okay. While Rob described the poor cell phone reception, he decided against sharing his experience of the blown tire and his wakeup call, saving that story for another time. Rachel said she understood that if Rob didn't call often, she knew why. Before ending the call, Rob offered a short prayer of gratitude for getting to the monastery reasonably safe and for Rachel's understanding, and closed with a simple goodnight and "I love you." After a deep breath, he looked at his watch and decided against going out to get a meal, remembering the half of a grilled chicken sandwich he had saved from a meeting earlier that day, and the remains of a large diet soda that would fit the bill. After finishing the leftover lunch, he prepared for bed and read through the Compline[3] service that he often enjoyed from his *Book of Common Prayer*,[4] barely making it through the evening prayers before dozing off.

CHAPTER 2
THE DAY OF SELF-AWARENESS AND LOOKING BACK

*"Let us not look back in anger, nor forward in fear,
but around in awareness."*
—James Thurber

When the bright sunlight flooded across his pillow and into his eyes, Rob realized that he had missed morning prayers in the chapel, as well as breakfast with the community. *Maybe I can find some leftovers,* he thought to himself. After personal care and dressing, he walked out into the hall with the idea of possibly finding some food in the monastery kitchen, but was pleasantly surprised to discover that the sisters had left him a quaint continental breakfast in the small kitchen of the guest house where he was staying. "Thank you!" he uttered for the kindness and generosity of the sisters' hospitality staff, now able to get some coffee and something to eat. The coffee was quite a bit better than he expected. He thought of the old television commercial where a husband remarked to his wife, "Honey, that's great coffee!", thinking that he might share this with the sisters, but quickly dismissed the thought.

Back in his room, or *Solitary,* as he considered naming it, he continued to enjoy the rest of his coffee after discovering that the small breakfast offerings were tasty and satisfying. Getting settled in the rocking chair with his journal and favorite pen, Rob began to reflect on what it was that brought him here, and what, perhaps, he now needed to examine after the event on the road and his trunk full of junk. Having known about the importance of doing a life review, Rob decided that this would be the time and place to start on at least an abbreviated reflection of his life, looking back to his early years, his education, his marriage and his career, and how, at times, he was forced to change along the way. He also realized he needed to admit how he had backslidden from who he was when he first came here to St. Cecilia's and grew in his three years in formation with the community. *Maybe,* he thought, *the trunk was just the tip of the iceberg.*

> *"Life is a culmination of the past, an awareness of the present, an indication of a future beyond knowledge, the quality that gives a touch of divinity to matter."* —Charles Lindbergh

Raised in the German and Italian neighborhoods of South St. Louis, with parents who survived The Great Depression and had served in WWII, Rob was taught to "waste not, want not" and to keep things that might be useful later. Not bad advice, it was tempered with not really having to want for much. While most of his childhood was unremarkable, the sudden death of his older sister Ann from a rare form of polio both shocked and stunned his family to the core. However, in some ways, it seemed to steel them, and with their Germanic and

English roots, the direction became one of keeping emotions on the down low while "keeping calm and carrying on." A few of Ann's belongings were kept, although hidden away in closeted boxes for many years. "We just have to keep going," he recalled his mother telling both he and his younger brother Phillip.

As boys, Rob and Phillip began collecting—with interesting finds like multi-colored rocks, odd nails, old coins, and any other items that might be considered "really old" or "valuable." Toys were kept until they broke. Baseball cards, comics, and magazines and brochures on motorcycles and cars emerged as the best items to collect, and then later it turned to record albums, posters, and some books in the teen years. Their dad had the usual business items, files, old record albums of his era, things saved from his time in the war, books, and a couple of well-loved chess sets. For their mom, family photos, scraps of paper for names and addresses, recipes, shopping lists, things she found interesting, newspaper and magazine articles and the like best seemed to fit the bill. Sometimes she would keep curious things like old calendars with no entries on them ("You know, in twenty years, this will be current again"),[1] or clean disposable food containers that commanded an even greater shelf space in the pantry than the food at times. Overall, though, the home was always in pretty good order, and the collections never seemed to get too far out of hand.

While Rob attended college at the large state university a couple of hours from home, before dropping out and enlisting in the Army, most of his belongings could fit in a car trunk and back seat. That might have been due to his meager number of possessions, or perhaps it was the limited amount of available space to store or move them. His parents, of course, kept a lot of things from his childhood—as parents do. However, in those years Rob felt little need to retrieve them.

In shipping off to boot camp, both the possessions and the available space became unavoidably smaller. For a few years it was limited to what would fit in his duffle bag and the limited space in his small '67 MG, which somehow managed to get he and his belongings transported between his duty stations as a medic. After a move or two of their own, his parents invariably "thinned" what was left at home, keeping only a few of his items. Later, some came to be seen as true treasures that were, in fact, very much worth keeping.

> *"Keep some souvenirs of your past, or how will you ever prove it wasn't all a dream?"* —Ashleigh Brilliant

Over almost three decades, having moved out on his own, starting and maintaining a sales career, after furnishing apartments and then homes, and then after his marriage—which doubled possessions stored at home—Rob became accustomed to a full house. While it did not include children, the new household consisted of himself, his spouse Meg, their 3 cats, and a Border Collie named Babe. There was also the necessary furniture and home appliances, clothing for both business and casual wear, televisions and stereo equipment, music and book collections, file cabinets and work materials, personal and business paperwork, photo albums, college papers and some things never thrown away from past jobs, kitchen utensils, small appliances, pots and pans, coffee makers and espresso machines, toasters, needed groceries, and so forth. Add in a few bicycles, yard tools, lawn mowers, a disorganized collection of needed tools, nails, nuts, and bolts, partially used kits from various home repairs and upgrades, etc., and then the garages and the basements soon succumbed to the ever-growing accumulation of things. Giving in to long-held desires and the need to "keep up with the Joneses," expensive health and beauty items, jewelry, finer clothes, and luxury watches soon took up their share of the space and the budget, along with the original display or shipping boxes from many of these items.

At the very apex of Rob's career, he was hammered with new losses and major disruptions. Although there had been hints and signs that change might be in the air, still there was no time to prepare, no transition period to break in the new reality. Some of the changes were too unexpected to benefit from any warning. These losses and disruptions—occurring and overlapping over a 48-month period— included the following: the departure of his wife Meg (who decided to leave the marriage, responding to an internal call and starting a new and different life on her own with Babe) and the subsequent divorce; the heartbreaking need to have the veterinarian euthanize their six-year-old cat Hemingway and to put the other two cats up for adoption; Rob's seemingly secure sales management position eliminated due to the company's downsizing; and the cleaning out and selling of their home in the Brookdale area of Kansas City, which had been the best home that he had known since childhood. Kicking all of this off was the devastating news from France of Phillip's sudden death due to a massive heart attack. Following a failed attempt at another relationship, spurred by Rob's deep, unrecognized, and unresolved grief, the wake-up calls rang even louder for him.

It was a time for discernment indeed, with a rude awakening from the blissful life that he had enjoyed and had taken for granted. There was the loss of the familiar and the routine, his brother's death, the divorce, the move, the disruption in his career and income, and the significant loss of a support system. Then his parents' difficult move to a nursing home due to their rapidly declining health. Within the year, both of them died.

That is when it really hit him—he was bereft of both a nuclear and an extended family. He was single, out of work, and without a place to call home—this was a place he had never been before. This was a desert experience—not of choice, but of circumstance. This was a new fierce landscape he had to accept, learn to navigate, and survive.

> *"What is necessary to change a person is to change his awareness of himself."* —Abraham Maslow

In the midst of this despair, he found he was unable to ignore the loud peal of the bells of these wake-up calls any more. Rob realized that he needed to focus on what was truly important. He began to take advantage of others' listening support, as well as his prayers, and decided to follow up with the referral to Father Jay. The one-time visit with the priest was brief, culminating with a gift to Rob of a copy of the *Book of Common Prayer*[2] along with a recommendation that he investigate the spiritual formation program at the Sophia Center. He didn't recall much in the way of any other specific instruction or guidance from the visit with Fr. Jay. He did, however, come away from it with a clear and hopeful vision that drove him straight to the program's website where he quickly applied and was enrolled.

Around the same time, two other opportunities surfaced for Rob within his church. One was a program that met weekly for 4 years, studying the Hebrew and Christian scriptures and church history. The group also engaged in theological reflection. The other opportunity was an invitation from another Episcopal priest, Fr. Woods. While Rob had at times lightly and only briefly considered joining a monastic order, this opportunity sounded too good to pass up. Ever since experiencing a mystical peak experience inspired by the incredible beauty of nature on an Easter Sunday morning at age seventeen, Rob had always felt an inner call to a deeper awareness, reverence, and connection to the Divine.

Fr. Woods had told Rob about the Order of St. Romanus,[3] a religious order that was based on the teachings and rule of St. Benedict, encouraging Rob to consider applying for admittance into the order as a Lay Associate. As such, Rob would become a "third order" member (after monks and nuns living in religious communities, who are considered as first and second religious orders). He would be out in the world, but not of it, and so would not be required to live a celibate life or reside within a monastery.

In a matter of weeks, Rob had investigated and quickly made application to all these programs and affiliations. He also knew that it would be a departure from his less-than-satisfying career in industrial sales—his new life would be that of spiritual formation, discovering and training for a different career, and hopefully transitioning into more meaningful work better aligned with the awakening he experienced by coming face to face with his grief.

So, this was his new life. Rob resigned from his job, leaving behind his heavy travel schedule and the often unpleasant job of selling and servicing industrial chemicals in the paper-converting business. He instead returned to his nursing background, working as a charge nurse in long-term care facilities.

Rob had now downsized his life, living as a single in a four-hundred-square foot studio apartment just off the Brookdale shopping district. This did not in any way reach the loftier career heights that he had once envisioned; it was now more of a lower base camp to regroup and to retool.

Rob continued his spiritual formation, downsized, thinned his possessions, and then enrolled in seminary, seeking specialization in education and in finding work as a spiritual care provider and healthcare chaplain in hospitals and hospice agencies. After his time of discernment, and having developed his personal Rule of Life, he was accepted by the Director of Associates and the other monks as a Lay Associate of the Order. So, there he was, part of a larger family, somewhat cloistered in his apartment, and with a salary about one-half of what he had received in sales. He was where he needed to be at this time in his life.

Then along came Rachel.

With six months of dating and premarital counseling under their belts after having been introduced by their mutual friend Debi, Rob and Rachel wed that next summer. The decision to move together into Rachel's three-bedroom home in the older suburbs was easy, although Rob had already grieved the loss of the small and simple studio apartment that had served him as a sort of "cocoon" in his transformation. The "what to keep" and "what to move" questions were fairly simple and didn't take either much thought or effort. As blessed as their new relationship was, Rob hadn't really anticipated all the complexities that invariably followed, including a new gestalt of schedules, requests, the assimilating and accommodating both of their lives along with existing combined belongings, and then the inevitable—but not anticipated—expansion of their accumulating even more together.

> *"A rich entrepreneur who lives a simple life with his family while helping as many people as he can, is more monk than a monk who lives a secluded life in a monastery meditating and begging."* —Abhijit Naskar, *Monk Meets World*

Happy in this new shared life, Rob was feeling a bit like he was before things had fallen apart those years before: work mastered, with a new healthcare ministry career and a stronger spiritual and grief support base, and in his having benefitted from the support of a six-week grief group in which he had participated. He was now enjoying a fuller life, with more things to manage and do at home, yet with a growing awareness of having less time for spiritual communion and contemplation. So what was the wake-up call *this* time?

The trunk!

Rob decided, after spending time immersing himself in nature in the areas in and around the monastery, that he would need to stay a while longer than he had anticipated. He had learned when he checked in that the guest room was available at least for the next three weeks, should he benefit from a longer retreat. Perhaps there was a new call being felt, and a new path required by this realization—a path not imposed by victimization, by outside circumstances such as had occurred in the previous wake-up call, but now one of his own doing. Rob began to see the fruits of things he had done and the things left undone; of commission and omission. With this, he made the decision to unpack his life.

Rob decided to take advantage of the sisters' offer to extend his stay, as well as the flexibility in his home and work schedule. Going outside, he found one spot on a nearby small hill where he could lock onto a cell tower signal, and called Rachel. After a lengthy phone call, in which he gained her understanding and her acceptance of his remaining at the monastery longer than he had planned, he arranged a two-week unpaid break from work and confirmed his extended stay as a silent retreat at St. Cecilia's. With the benefit of the weekends, he had now garnered a full two weeks, plus two weekends, to stay and write. He drove the several blocks into town, had the tire replaced at Brad's Automotive, and after buying some pizza and a bottle of wine from a nearby convenience store, returned to his room, finished off a few pieces of pizza with of glass of wine, did some reading, brushed his teeth, and crawled into bed.

CHAPTER 3
THE NEXT MORNING; THE JOURNAL BEGINS

"Journaling is paying attention to the inside for the purpose of living well from the inside out."
—Lee Wise

With sunlight streaming in, Rob awoke and realized that he had again missed morning prayers with the sisters and the breakfast that followed. He wondered if the continental breakfast might be available in the small kitchen and common area. After some silent prayers he dressed and walked back to where he had found the offerings yesterday. To his relief and with his gratitude, he peered over the morning treats and beverages and helped himself to a few items that looked good, along with the sisters' most excellent coffee. *Maybe*, he thought, *this will become my new morning practice. It may not be a spiritual practice, but I'll not only be filled with food but also with gratitude.* And while it looked like a beautiful day outside the kitchen window, ideal for a walk, Rob decided to return to his room, realizing that he first needed to call Sister Evelyn in the center's office. Stepping outside, he was able to get a signal and reached her at the office number. After confirming availability and accepting their offer of accommodations for an extended stay, he got approval to use their Wi-Fi as needed for his access to the internet. Seating himself in the chair by the desk, he quickly got online and set up the announcement on his email server to notify all others that he would not be able to answer emails over the next two weeks or so. His notebook and laptop now beckoned him to the work that lie ahead.

Why do we collect and hold onto things? he asked himself. With this, a plan slowly took shape. Every morning he would greet the day with prayers as he took a meditative walk around the grounds. When he returned, he would have breakfast from the guest kitchen area and then return to his cell. The rest of the morning would be spent reading from some of his favorite books that he had brought along for the retreat, including books by Margaret Guenther, Richard Rohr, Cynthia Bourgeault, and Ron Rolheiser. For lunch, he would support one of the local pizza or sub sandwich restaurants, buying enough for both his lunch and each evening's meal that he would keep in the refrigerator in the kitchen area. When he was out, he would also occasionally pick up a 12-pack of bottled water and a bottle or two of a decent wine. Each afternoon would include some time to talk with Sr. Margaret, his available and wonderful spiritual director, for the personal spiritual companioning where they would together discern the subtle—or the obvious—movements of God in Rob's life. He would take time for solitude and journaling at the nearby wooded lakeside area where he had always found respite in nature and a spot for reflection. Each evening would be full enough with his typing up his notes and reflections in his journal, enjoying his dinner of the leftovers from lunch, a glass of wine, and showering before going to bed. *A lot of work is ahead*, he realized, as he began to grasp the breadth and depth of this effort. Although in the past he had often been able to write about 800-900 words per day in his journaling, he estimated that this work might require up to 1,500 words per day. Unpacking the unnecessary—personal downsizing—needed to be predicated on some serious reflection and contemplation, on his working through a series of questions and listening for their answers.

> *"Writing is medicine. It is an appropriate antidote to injury. It is an appropriate companion for any difficult change."* —Julia Cameron

This problem was not to be solved with some simple action comparable to calling one of the "1-800-Go-Trash"[1] companies that were always advertising; this would involve some real work to look "under" the possessions, clutter, and trash. With this in mind, Rob seated himself at the small oak desk in his cell, opened his laptop, and began to type …

OK cell, here I am. What do you have to teach me? I look around the room and see the pieces of furniture and a few things on the wall. I begin to think about how and why we collect and use things. This room is simple. Being here reminds me of the nice feeling I always get when checking into a newly cleaned hotel room, with no clutter, just nice furnishings, clear countertops, an empty closet, and a made bed. Why is it that we can't live this way at home all the time? This is an easy question to ask, but a difficult one to answer.

So, the junk in my trunk was a wake-up call. I am starting to realize that there is much more to this than just holding a lot of junk in my car's trunk, which caused me to commit to this extended retreat.

What I really think I want to explore here is threefold: first, how it is that we collect things—both consciously and unconsciously—to help us make sense of our lives; secondly, why and how we process the feelings of grief from the people and the things that we've lost through our collections and recollections; and lastly, discovering and committing to new ways in which we can simplify our lives, sort through the meaningful, and grow in the experience.

Prior to the tire blowout, I had thought about this for some time, after recently having given a presentation to a group of grief professionals regarding collections and grief. I had reflected about how men (more often than women) often restore an old car, perhaps a model similar to one that their father owned, or one that was symbolic of their youth or a special time in their life. Some men will treasure their dad's tools or fishing and hunting gear. After such a talk on men and grief, one man came up to me after the presentation and smiled as he shared how he had kept and treasured his dad's fishing rods, reels, hooks, and lures. I realized also, having heard many stories and examples, that many women (more typically than men) will keep, collect, and often add to their mother's or grandmother's collections of china, quilts, or glassware, as well as other things like lace, silverware, and jewelry. Does this have something to do with nostalgia? Are these things considered keepsakes, heirlooms, or something similar? I began to understand that much of it may have its origins in wanting to remember and hold dear memories of times, places, lost youth, and particularly our dearly departed loved ones. Collecting and treasuring items are a way to honor and be loyal to those whom we loved (and continue to love). Some of us, in addition to the various ways of feeling and expressing our feelings, may go beyond collecting and keeping material things to the cognitive and behavioral grief work of taking action—creating or building something as a tribute to loved ones, as a memorial, or as a way to serve others—following in their loved one's footsteps, so to speak. Many of us will plant a tree, create a garden, or donate a bench; some of us start a foundation, or participate in fundraisers for causes related to our loved ones in some way.

Yes, having furniture and cars and refrigerators and books are all things that we find that we need and enjoy. But what is it that makes us keep something that a grandparent owned, or a collection of rocks, baseball cards, dolls or action figures, or a ticket to a concert that we attended decades ago? Why do we hold onto a collection of stamps, an autograph, or a baby's lock of hair? And why do we keep a broken vase, a subway token, or clothes that no longer fit?

It comes down to these three concepts: Connection. Belonging. Meaning.

JOURNALING GUIDE FOR PART 1: WAKING UP
CHAPTERS 1–3

Journaling Guide for Part I: Waking Up (chapters 1-3)

1. What led me to buy this book? What "spoke" to me about it?
2. What do I hope to learn, to do, and to be from having read this book and doing the journaling?
3. When have I taken a trip that "woke me up" and changed my life?
4. In what ways was I changed through that experience?
5. Looking back, I will journal about some of the times when I responded to "wake-up calls," and the times when I ignored or pushed them away.
6. I will describe a time when I realized that a brief retreat or vacation wasn't quite long enough, and I really needed more time.
7. In what ways have I been encumbered or possessed by my possessions?
8. Where do I see that I have too much stuff around me that is no longer needed, holds unpleasant memories,

or takes away space from the more pleasant, joyful, and meaningful things in my life?

PART TWO
FACING UP

CHAPTER 4
THE "WHYS" AND THE "WHATS" OF COLLECTING AND KEEPING

> *"It is preoccupation with possessions, more than anything else, that prevents us from living freely and nobly."*
> —Bertrand Russell

I am back in my solitary cell after my morning prayers, walk, and breakfast, and am now seated again at the small desk in my cell. I had found a newer office chair that was in an unused room down the hall, and quickly replaced my room's straight-back wooden chair with it, figuring that a padded one should be much more comfortable. With no television or radio, I now have no excuse to not get started. And while I have my cell phone, I am not a person who does much on it besides calls or texts. Besides, I am feeling quite motivated to look deeper into the matter of possessions, grief, purpose, connection, belonging, and meaning.

What I am wondering now is how we classify or categorize our things, or our "stuff." I will admit that the "collection" that I had in my trunk was pretty much stuff that I needed to give away, throw away, or recycle. Those things which are not really needed or valued, I could truly describe as "junk." But what about our things that are above that level — from the "I'm just holding onto this for..." to the "I'll never part with this because ..." level? How do we name these, and does it help to label them as being part of a group or a collection? Let's give it a try.

TERMS, CONCEPTS, AND DEFINITIONS

Artifact: an object made by human beings, perhaps being especially historical or significant.

Asset: property, valuables, holdings, inventory, etc.

Collecting: the act of gathering, of bringing together; accumulating, amassing, storing, and grouping similar things.

Collection: a gathering or grouping of things, a reserve or inventory of holdings; often, but not always purposeful.

Commemorate: to celebrate, acknowledge, remember, show respect for, or to pay tribute to another or an event.

Future Use: preparing for a time to come, or a prospective or intended use, forward in time.

Heirloom: something of value due to its emotional significance, as in objects kept and handed down within a family.

Inventory: like assets, as in stock, holdings, or some reserve of objects or items, recorded in type, category, and/or number.

Junk: things which are useless, meaningless, or of little value to the beholder.

Keepsake: something kept as a reminder from an event, person, or a special time.

Memento: like a keepsake, an object to remind one of something or someone from the past.

Memorialist: someone who writes, constructs, or performs a memorial or a tribute to someone or something.

Memorialize: to preserve the memory of someone or something.

Nostalgia/nostalgic: a sentimental longing or wistful affection for a time, place, or state of being from the past.

Possession: something one owns, keeps, or has in their control, with varying degrees of value, consisting of anything from junk to jewels.

Relic: a physical object or substance that is believed, or felt, to have or hold part of the essence of something or someone from the past, usually considered as being much more real than symbolic, and often held in very high regard as something truly set apart or even holy.

Remembering: having and holding in one's mind and heart, in thoughts and feelings; recalling mentally and at times emotionally; to call to mind, recollect, think of, or look back on.

Sentimental: of feelings or views, usually of sadness, tenderness, or nostalgia; often romantic feelings are present.

Souvenirs: something that helps one recall the past, often from places or events.

Stuff: an "uncountable noun" that can be used for any variety or category of things.

Trash: refuge or garbage; items or materials that are no longer needed or valuable that have been or should be discarded.

That list might seem exhausting, but I wanted my "collection" of terms to be, well, a good collection.

Distinctions need to be made, perhaps, of how each person consciously or unconsciously names or groups their possessions. How do we assign value to items? Do we decide in a cognitive or some other way? Is our process emotional? Is it psychological, based on deep-seated or unconscious purposes? Let's take a closer look at the "why" and the "what."

THE WHY

Mentally, we will view our decisions as rational, intentional, practical, and purposeful. We use those factors in choosing to buy, pick up, or hold on to something. If there are emotional motives behind our reasoning and actions, we may be influenced by good (or bad) memories, pleasure, greed or fear, joy, sadness, or for the purpose of honoring someone else who is no longer in our lives. Psychologically, our actions may arise out of attempts to counter or mediate anxiety or depression, or something related to our earlier life (think of "Rosebud" in the film Citizen Kane[1]). As well, psychological collecting may progress to the point where a person's relationship shifts from the person or thing that they are remembering to the object itself. Grief also plays a large part here as well, which I hope to expand upon in my coming journal musings.

What about things of utility versus a collection? Is owning a lot of shirts, sweaters, or pairs of socks comparable to a collection of Star Wars action figures? Having a nice set of china may be both useful and very valued, but what if you own three sets of them? Would you say that you are a collector of china? I have a friend who married a man who had a good portion of the basement dedicated to his fishing gear, rods and reels, lures, and tackle boxes. He had inherited some of it and continued to add to what we would easily consider a collection. He treasured it; she saw it as a "waste of space." For someone who loves to fish, they may have their reasons for having each piece. Likewise, a guitarist can explain why they have a dozen guitars, and a chef can quickly explain the benefit derived from each piece of cookware. These examples may blur the lines between utility and art (or passion), and so these might be categorized as collections of utility, profession, artistry, or hobby.

THREE CATEGORIES OF OUR REASONS

The major reasons for collecting, saving, and retaining can all fit within one or more of these three categories: the mostly rational reasons, the mostly emotional ones, and those which are mostly subconscious.

When we find ourselves giving an explainable—or rational—reason for collecting or refusing to let something go, it most likely falls in this group. Reasons such as, "I need it because ..." or "This is a family heirloom," or "I can resell this at a huge profit," or "It was 30% off!" are probably helpful in justifying to ourselves why we are buying or holding on to something. We may be trying to convince ourselves or others of the soundness of our decisions. Holding onto a calendar for over twenty years because at some point the dates on it will realign with a future year is such a rationalization.

When feelings are a contributing factor (whether voiced or not), what would most likely be heard or thought are things like "I want it ..." or "It makes me feel good" or something like "I just have to keep it ... it was my grandmother's, and she loved it." Keeping things as conscious reminders of the past, or even those things that remind us of what or who we hoped to become at some point, would also fit here.

The third group—the subconscious or unconscious—will be easily recognizable with statements like "There's just something about it," "I'm not sure why, but ...", or "I just can't seem to part with it!"

TEN EVEN MORE WAYS TO CLASSIFY OUR PATTERNS AND OUR PROBLEMATIC PLACES

1. *"This is what I watched and learned growing up!"*
2. *"I have so much available space!"; or "That room looks too empty!"*
3. *"I'm a saver!"; "Waste not, want not" (especially with having had parents who lived through the Great Depression)*
4. *Bargain shopper; survivalist or "prepper"; stockpiling; "shopaholic"; or in having "proof" of one's abundance and prosperity*
5. *Environmentally conscious ("I don't want to add that to the landfill!") or "expenditure aware" ("I no longer wear it ... but I paid good money for that!")*
6. *Resulting from life's changes and transitions (upsizing or downsizing; divorced or widowed)*
7. *The "leave behinds" (from parents, ex-spouses, partners, former roommates, etc.)*
8. *"Hopelessly sentimental" (of loved ones, past good times, heirlooms, photos, etc.)*
9. *Grief-based (especially in situations of prolonged grief and unfinished relationships, and in not being able to part with things due to the pain of grief)*
10. *Having limited abilities and resources to manage one's accumulations and clutter; hoarding disorder; or a general inability to manage clutter, junk mail, trash, etc.*

Should a distinction be made between "collecting" and "hoarding"? Of course. Hoarding is now diagnosable and is included as a disorder in the DSM-5,[2] the reference manual for the diagnosis of mental illness and behavioral disorders. It is perfectly normal to buy and keep things, or to let things accumulate, of course, but as in many situations, the distinction is in the amount, frequency, or the degree of joy and happiness it all provides, or how much personal distress or difficulty it causes self or others. I don't want to focus too much on hoarding disorder; it may be helpful here, however, to recognize it as something on the far end of a continuum or spectrum, whether rational, emotional, or subconscious (or through a mental disorder or a physical disability), or simply from the inability to deal with excessive accumulation, clutter, and/or trash.

As we look further at reasons for collecting or keeping, wherever we fall on the spectrum, it might be helpful to list several underlying needs or desires:

FOR BUYING OR COLLECTING ... Necessity, enjoyment, future use, greed, power, anxiety avoidance, enjoyment, self-image or self-esteem, remembering others, shared interests, and connections with others through group membership, etc. I could go on and on ...

For saving or holding onto ... All the above and more, such as denial, anxiety, fear, looking back more than being in the present or in looking forward, remembrance and loyalty, nostalgia, sentimentality, procrastination, things long paid off, poor self-control, habituation, and a creeping lack of awareness over the amount or the value of possessions, junk, or trash.

So, in summary, here's something to consider asking ourselves: What is it that either 1) motivates me to collect or hold onto possessions, or 2) detracts, prevents, or holds me back from possession/clutter management?

THE WHAT

What sort of things do we collect and keep? There are, of course, many things that we collect and hold on to that are nontangible—less-than-helpful thoughts and emotions. We may be hoarding anger, regrets, the inability to forgive, trauma, negative self-talk, and painful memories. Conversely, we may have collected positive and helpful emotions—joy, peace, comfort, healing, positive self-talk, and good memories. And while we may have the potential to grow from the negative nontangibles, most would argue that it feels better—and is healthier—to collect and hold on to the positive ones. In regard to the tangibles (which often influence our thoughts and feelings) we can group these objects as things of differing value: some are treasured, and some are practical; some are sentimental, and some have monetary value. Looking back at the past nostalgically through "rose-colored glasses" is quite valuable for many. Still others may value objects of tribute, loyalty, honor, and grief. These can move us forward through what is referred to as "transformative grief."

What about these? Art, autographs, baseball cards, cassette tapes, audio CDs (and 8-track tapes, anyone?), Barbie dolls, Beanie Babies, beer cans, books, coins, comic books, decorative items, glassware, HotWheels cars, jewelry, political buttons, old license plates, ornaments, quilts, stamps, sports memorabilia, Precious Moments and Hummel figurines, postcards, record albums, silverware, tattoos, and so forth? With regard to photos: while most of us find it perfectly sensible and desirable—and even of critical importance—to keep photographs from our lives, there are some that collect old photographs from other people's lives. I had a neighbor once who had amassed quite an incredible collection of vintage photographs of people that he didn't know. What we really need to decide is why it is that we keep these things. We need to be truly honest with *ourselves so that we can decide what we need to keep, what has value for us, and what no longer serves a purpose.*

It has been said that to remember is to "re-member," or to recall, reconnect, or to make efforts to bring back the missing thing or person into our life or family. Should someone happen to find their self on a deserted island or struggling to survive as a refugee or as someone trapped in a war zone with nothing but some minimal access to clothes, food, and shelter, they would, of course, mentally remember their prior life and what and whom they no longer have in the present. They would have few items or photos to touch or look at in their recalling and remembering. For the rest of us who are fortunate enough to not be in that situation, we are blessed to have access to the things that do help in our recollection, such as photos and the other types of objects that I listed above.

We would be best served, however, to understand that the items are simply links to our memories. They are not, however, the person or the love that we are missing. They may represent the other, or help us to remember them, yet they are not the other. I have been often told by those with whom I have worked that certain objects, pieces of clothing, etc., are being kept and treasured because the other person "wore it" or "touched it." I have worked with some people who have experienced considerable difficulty in parting with things by refusing to let go of an artifact, piece of clothing, or a half-used bottle of cologne, because the loved one bought it, touched it, or wore it. These things remind us of the other. More than a few people have even told me that for them to throw out anything would be "disloyal" to the other. Whether they left on their own volition, or passed away, they probably wouldn't care what you keep or throw away. Further, any good book on dealing with a loved one's personal possessions will tell you that it's perfectly fine to keep a select number of items of another's to treasure. Rachel Kodanaz does a wonderful job of giving examples of culling another's possessions from her personal life and others in her book, Finding Peace, One Piece at a Time.[3] *For example, you might consider letting go of another's clothing through sharing and donating but keeping a few special items. In her book,* Passed and Present,[4] *Allison Gilbert provides several fun and creative suggestions (and resources) for repurposing meaningful and special objects as you thin the rest. My wife Rachel, for instance, has a quilt that is made from her father's tie collection. Hospice volunteers with whom I worked became skilled at creating lovely pillows for family members from their loved one's favorite shirt or a military uniform. These are creative and sometimes fun ways to remember someone in a way that is also practical.*

> "Anything you cannot relinquish when it has outlived its usefulness possesses you, and in this materialistic age a great many of us are possessed by our possessions." —Peace Pilgrim

Here are some tasks or things I think it is important to consider:

Know the terms and the definitions ... Define what it is that you are faced with and need to do—with reasons and explanations—and name it ... For things to possess and care for positively, perhaps consider the imperative, "Name it, claim it, and frame it" ... For feeling better about collecting and possessing, maybe this would work: "Name it, claim it, and re-frame it" ... And for those things which we know (or are told) that we need to let go of: "Give it a name, accept the blame, and release the shame." We can still hold onto the love while lightening the load.

CHAPTER 5
THE REWARDS OF OBTAINING, COLLECTING, ACCUMULATING, AND HOLDING ON TO THINGS

> *"The best way to find out what we really need is to get rid of what we don't. Quests to faraway places or shopping sprees are no longer necessary. All you have to do is eliminate what you don't need by confronting each of your possessions properly."*
> —Marie Kondo

This is my sixth day here, and I am realizing just how easy it is to get caught up in my writing. During the past two days I needed to delve deeply into the what and the why of collecting and possessions. To give it justice, I needed a lot of words to describe what I saw when I really looked at it closely. So, today I am starting in on the journal earlier after my morning routine. Having already made a call and left a voicemail for Rachel, I hope to get out into nature and perhaps visit with Sister Margaret sometime later today after my journaling.

I think it is important that I begin this reflection on intentional, purposeful collecting. I can see a variety of underlying reasons—

practical, relational, emotional, psychosocial, and spiritual. There are also the neuroanatomical rewards from pleasure centers in the brain, activated or stimulated by the anticipation of the reward from the neurotransmitter dopamine. It has been suggested that the anticipation of a reward or a benefit rates even higher in the brain then the acquisition of the reward or benefit itself. Perhaps I could list the rewards according to general categories, but this is not necessary. Individuals most assuredly rate or value rewards quite individually, with any number of variables. However, broad categories that affect reward motivation could be considered, beginning with the most basic and universal.

First, there is the fulfilling of needs for simply practical reasons or motivations. Buying groceries, toilet tissue, or school supplies isn't typically viewed as something to be enjoyed or looked forward to. We buy and keep things that we need to live our lives. If we are able to access resources for food, water, shelter, healthcare, and other base needs, it is crucial and life sustaining to be able to get the things that we require to live.

Next, there are the things that we use but also look forward to, as they bring us some enjoyment or satisfaction. Some examples might be purchasing new electronic devices (one of my joys, which I can always justify) or buying new shoes (which Rachel can always justify), as well as collecting music, movies, or books. These can be both fun and beneficial. As well, we experience feelings of satisfaction, joy, connection, and meaning through our possessions, which often include things of remembrance, such as heirlooms and keepsakes. In a way, these things help us to transcend time and space with those who have gone before. The "invisible string" of continuing bonds keeps us connected and in relationship with those loved ones.

Then there are the things that we purchase, save, or collect for the purpose of future use, such as our savings, 401K plans, investments, or even continuing education through college or technical school and ongoing professional development—things that we expect will benefit us in the coming days. This very much describes me. Rachel is quick to point out that I seem to like collecting certificates to fill up the wall space. For me, however, lifelong learning, advancing my education, and attaining certifications in my field are all motivating and rewarding. Through them, I experience satisfaction and validation through setting and reaching both my "performance" and my "mastery" goals: performance goals for the grade and the certificate, and mastery goals for the joy of mental growth and expansion of skills. Personally, I see these as complementary to my "be-ing needs" on Abraham Maslow's hierarchy of needs.[1] Similarly, those of us who are savers benefit from both the motivation and the rewards from seeing our savings or retirement accounts grow, in turn giving us a sense of future security as opposed to anxiety or worry. In effect, greater peace of mind.

There are also many who collect things of value primarily because they are unique, rare, valuable, or exquisitely beautiful—like various artwork, sports memorabilia, jewelry, precious metals, or original paintings—for reasons that may include enjoyment, status, and power, or their expected future value for later resale at a profit. These motivations and rewards can easily overlap, as is the case with art and beauty and money. Sometimes they may involve a "touch with greatness," such as in owning works of art from a well-regarded artist, celebrity autographs, or signed footballs from a championship team. These may also include some transcendent qualities in evidencing our own lives as interconnected with others from the past or from figures of greatness. For some, it might be realized from owning an authentic letter signed by President Abraham Lincoln; for another, it might be a prized home run baseball hit by Hank Aaron. Some of these rewards are more "intrinsic," that is, internal or personally meaningful within us, and others "extrinsic," as something from the outside of us, or material. Examples of the extrinsic might be objects of beauty that others envy or regard highly, things which increase our self-esteem or worth in others' opinions, or items or property that gives us a hope of future gain. For intrinsic, we might think of those things which bring us inner joy, peace, satisfaction, a sense of belonging, mastery, or connection with others or the divine. In my life, for instance, I value those extrinsic things like the few autographed books that I own, as well as feeling intrinsic rewards from being able to contribute to a charitable organization or in helping another who needs a favor or a kind word. Earning a degree or completing a course with a good grade may reward me both extrinsically and intrinsically.

> "We are not the sum of our possessions." —George H. W. Bush

Finally, here, at this juncture, is where I feel that our big needs for connection, belonging, and meaning come together: through the awareness and the work of grief, and the growth that is possible through transformation and transcendence.

> "I think all kinds of meanings in life transcend your self. They're linked to other generations of people around us, to our children and our family. We're passing on something of ourselves to others. I feel that's what makes our life full of meaning." —Irvin D. Yalom

CHAPTER 6
CHANGE = LOSS = GRIEF

"There is nothing permanent except change."
—Heraclitus

If I am reading the calendar correctly, this is my seventh day here. The weather has been nice, although I haven't really been out much. The few hours that I've spent in the park have been pleasant—immersed in nature, surrounded by trees and with a pastoral view of the lake. It is time away from things made by humans, yet still time to reflect on those people and things far from here. Some of those people and things are long gone from my sight—past friendships and broken relationships, separation by divorce, and the deaths of loved ones. There are the places of safety and comfort from the past—homes, good jobs, great co-workers, and fun vacations. In retrospect, there are the times of my life growing up, some captured in photographs and others etched in my memories—receiving loving care as a child, growing in trust and with a sense of autonomy and increasing competence. My adolescence saw the growth of closer relationships with friends, with an increasing independence and a stronger self-identity. Then there were the years of college as a young adult, developing my career, and forming ever more and deeper intimate relationships and friendships. With the middle adulthood years came increased generativity, marriage, a professional career, and opportunities to give back through non-profit volunteer leadership.

Here's the rub: All through life we are taught to gain, to acquire, to become autonomous, capable, and social. To get good grades, to make friends, to get a diploma, and, for many of us, a degree. To land a good job, get married, have children, establish a career, and make money. We are not taught about—or guided on how to prepare for—the time when we no longer have those special people, places, things, or times in our lives. When we no longer have that special someone or something significant in our life, we realize that we no longer possess them—if we ever did in the first place—and we experience it as loss. We are taught to get, to take, to have, to earn, to win. We are not taught to let go of, to give away, to let someone else earn, or to lose. Remember: "Change = loss = grief." Thus, any change—not just the huge loss of the death of a loved one—can result in a sense of loss, and thus the need to grieve that loss.

The Grief Recovery Institute, which runs the Grief Recovery Method groups, explains grief this way: "Grief is the natural and normal reaction to a significant loss of any kind or a change in a familiar pattern of behavior."[1] *Even when young, whether you are experiencing the death of a pet or the death of an elderly grandparent, whether you have to move away from friend, or leave one school to start at another school—all these things are changes and therefore losses.*

Here's a story that I need to share from one of my earliest memories: When my mom took me to my first day of kindergarten at the grade school near our house, I had just turned five and had never been outside the care of my parents or grandparents. The image of my mom waving to me from the other side of the glass partition by the closed door to this day remains a vivid memory for me. Being that young age, I really couldn't understand it. Other than some occasional oversight by my grandparents, there was no such thing as day care or preschool. My whole life up to this point consisted primarily of home, family, and playing with my sister, my brother Phillip, and our dog Rascal. I can't say for sure if I felt abandoned as I watched my mom wave goodbye to me on that first day of kindergarten. However, I did see it as a big change in a familiar and safe pattern of behavior and routine. Once I was able to grasp it and adjust, I became okay with it, and pretty much walked myself to school throughout the rest of grade school and high school until I was old enough to drive. I came to see my teachers as caring and competent. I learned that I could trust others outside of my immediate family. I had suffered my first loss, yet I gained in independence and trust. And while that really didn't prepare me for my family's great loss when my big sister Ann died less than a year later, I'm pretty sure that the earlier loss gave me a foundation of awareness that loss is a part of life. I also believe that my having experienced losses and grief, along with support and love, helped ease my transition from home to college some twelve years later.

So, these times and places, these changes, these people who disappear from our lives—when they are past and gone, they are the losses and the changes we need to grieve. We also grieve the things that we have associated with these people, places, things, and times. When I began to really study this several years ago, I realized that we usually come to treasure those reminders of who—and what— we no longer have with us in life. As I interviewed others in preparing for a presentation that I recently gave to a group of grief support specialists, I found that many had kept—as did I—not only photos, but many treasured items that their parents and their grandparents had collected and held onto, such as quilts, china, silverware, tools, fishing & hunting gear, older cars, the family home, and so forth. As well, more than a few had kept some of their own childhood toys, dolls, lunchboxes, action figures, Matchbox or HotWheels cars, etc., or had tried to later find replacements for them online or in antique malls.

I need to look no further than recalling my study back home, where —in addition to my books, a favorite old desk, and an antique wardrobe—I have several reminders, treasured keepsakes, photos, and mementos. From memory, let me give you a quick guided tour ... The first thing one would probably notice as they walk into my study is the large, beautiful oak wardrobe. I bought the piece, estimated to be around 120 years old, from the previous owner of the house in Brookdale. I have other pieces of furniture, such as some library bookcases, an old desk and an office chair that I bought at a thrift shop, and two comfy chairs for reading. And books? Yes, of course! Several hundred books across the categories of theology, spirituality, leadership, coaching, aging, history, grief, Indigenous studies, pastoral care, ethics, and management among others. On occasion I will thin these to make room for new ones. One of the chairs—a quite handsome piece in a durable tan leather—is especially significant for me, as I bought it from a dear friend and colleague when he downsized and moved to California. Not only is it attractive and comfortable, what makes it special is that it had belonged to my friend. I also have a cherry secretary that was a gift from the family of dear friends some years before, for whom I had provided spiritual support while they were in their 90s. I had also helped the family clean out and prepare the home for sale after the couple's deaths. I think of them each time I use the secretary. Two of the bookcases came from a nearby Episcopal church that had been decommissioned and sold. Like the three auditorium seats from a remodeling at Mount St. Cecilia, these were also rescued and are now some of my favorite furniture pieces. As one looks around, it would be hard *not to notice all of the photographs and framed certificates—group photos of people with whom I have attended school, served in the military and worked with, and certificates and diplomas from high school, college, graduate schools, and various training programs. There are a couple of recognition pieces—from volunteer leadership positions from my careers, and from my alma maters. There are numerous photos—on bookshelves and stuck between the glass panes of the secretary doors—of my family, friends, coworkers, colleagues, and other authors I have been lucky enough to meet. I have an icon that was painted by my Benedictine nun friend, Sister Trinitas, presented as a gift to me over 40 years ago. There are two Hawaiian Ti plants near a window that I had started from a souvenir "log" from a trip to Knotts Berry farm in California after my college graduation. My dad's old brass desk calendar that flips to show each new day sits on a shelf. As a memorial some years back, I set it to December 8th, commemorating John Lennon's life and his tragic death. I have various small stones on shelves from travels to the desert Southwest, and on an opposite bookshelf, model cars of the automobiles that my parents owned, as well as those of my own early cars. I'm sure that nearly every one of us has our own personal collection and displays of things and remembrances of those special people, places, things, and times in our lives.*

> "People lose people, we lose things in our life as we're constantly growing and changing. That's what life is—change, and a lot of that is loss. It's what you gain from that loss that makes life."
> —Thomas Jane

In my work as a chaplain and grief specialist, I saw how the people I talked with and listened to recalled and shared stories of their favorite items from childhood. I realized that these possessions were tremendously instrumental in our processing our lives and in naming and attempting to reclaim what and whom we missed. In effect, the toys and artifacts from their earlier lives became their reminders and touchstones. The things that had belonged to those who have gone on before are now their things—they are the new caretakers and guardians for these objects, symbolic and representative of earlier times and loved ones, gone but not forgotten. Boys' and girls' toys had, in fact, become the men's and women's "lens" for a sharper and wider view of growth and transcendence, providing a 10,000-foot look at their lives. I was experiencing this new view from my own losses, and saw that others were experiencing their own as well.

So—what am I to do now with this insight?

CHAPTER 7
THE WORK

> *"Knowing is not enough; we must apply.*
> *Willing is not enough; we must do."*
> —Johann Wolfgang von Goethe

Back from my prayers, breakfast, and a walk around the grounds, I am now seated back at my desk in my "cell." A brief call to Rachel confirmed something we thought might be in the works, in that her friend JoAnna was able to stop over from her trip from LA to New York so they could spend some time together and catch up. That takes a bit of pressure off from me, as I know they can enjoy this time together while I am here. As for my time at St. Cecilia's, I am feeling like I am back on track, following what I created as an outline for sorting through it all. I am finding that the more I discover and write, the more comes to heart and mind. I do plan to continue with my daily routine, yet I can also see that my hours of writing have been increasing. This reminds me of the diligence that I've always put into anything that I set out to do, as well as experiencing those times of "flow" where I get so absorbed in my work that time seems to fly by. So, today's topic is work—the work of *collecting, sorting, keeping, and letting go of the varied material things. This may be a needed part of the work of grief, yet it is also needed to fulfill our personal desire for some degree of minimalism through the downsizing and "rightsizing" in our lives and our personal environment.*

Several years ago, an older friend had expressed to me how shocked and angry she was when she learned that her older brother's daughter cleaned out her father's home shortly after he had died. My friend and the other family members weren't notified of the daughter's intention and actions. Apparently, she ordered a dumpster, and everything in the home, other than perhaps a few items the daughter wanted for herself, was tossed into the dumpster and sent to a landfill. Family photos, furniture, heirlooms, as well as worn-out clothes, the mundane, and the trash. were all gone. Perhaps this met the daughter's needs, but certainly not those of my friend nor the rest of the family.

On the other end of the spectrum there is the story of a client's father who never threw anything out, never downsized belongings, and even got to the point of being unable to clean up after the pet birds and cats or to take out the trash. Newspapers, magazines, and food wrappers were everywhere; walking paths in the house had all but disappeared.

In one situation, a radical purging; in the other, a pathological avoidance or inability. For the first, there may have been impatience, avoidance of pain, or a deliberate decision to not involve the family in going through their loved one's possessions. For the second, perhaps some level of fear, laziness, physical inability, or a habituated blindness to even see the piles of stuff and trash. Either way is not recommended.

For the rest of us, we are aware that over time we seem to accumulate more and more, and it really takes some dedicated effort to control it. More paper—in the form of various mailings—comes into the house than goes out; new clothes are purchased, but the older ones aren't faithfully donated or thrown out. Newer electronic devices, appliances, toys, games, books, magazines, tools, etc., are bought, yet the older ones, along with their associated cords, adapters, parts, etc., often remain somewhere in the house or garage, in closets and drawers, and are not donated, recycled, or disposed of with environmental consciousness.

Maybe it was something drilled into me in the military, but I like a clean, uncluttered home and work area. In those rare times when I travel and check into a hotel, I can feel myself relax when I walk into a clean room with clear countertops and no clutter. There is plenty of open space, and so it is much easier to find something you might be looking for when there is fewer other things lying on top that could be hiding it. When Rachel is looking for something that she has misplaced and laments, "I've looked all over for it and I still can't find it!" I know that it's most likely under something else. I feel like responding, "Have you looked all under for it?" which I know she may see as a wise answer, but not an amusing one.

So, keeping up takes effort. When I had begun earlier to think about the monastic life, I envied for some time those entering a community, envisioning their making a clean break of downsizing (or rightsizing) their lives. I imagined their discarding their old life and possessions, entering the monastery like the proverbial camel going through the "eye of a needle" (perhaps referencing the small doorways for entering the Temple in Jerusalem or other edifices)[1]*—that is, on their knees, unburdened, with nothing on their backs. Perhaps dropping everything, leaving everything behind, would not be so difficult at age 20, but considerably more difficult after age 50.*

So, we live along a continuum, from keeping nothing (or throwing out everything), to keeping everything. We are all probably some-

where on the spectrum of hoarding. The admonition, "all things in moderation," may be wise indeed, but how do we find that sweet spot on our continuum—what is best for us? I like to look at the pros and the cons in terms of my sense of peace or comfort. I have to ask myself, "Does my environment feel more peaceful or more disturbing? Do I feel more comfortable or uncomfortable with the number of things that I keep in my life? Do my habits in managing my possessions help or hurt others?" We can both feel pleasure and comfort from collecting and holding onto things, yet also from cleaning house and getting rid of things. We have our reasons of connection, belonging, meaning, and even monetary profit. We are motivated both by pleasure and pain, not in an "only one or the other" sort of way, but rather, on a continuum. So, like many other things, it is personal, situational, and contextual. Tossing out a gift that you never liked from a second cousin whom you rarely see would probably be much easier than letting go of a similar gift from a best friend or your partner. Whether we're keeping something or letting it go, we must also ask ourselves—for whom are we really doing it?

"The beginning is the most important part of the work." —Plato

I had learned earlier in business school the concept of the cost/benefit analysis. The work of collecting, keeping, and letting go of items can utilize this framework as well. Let me explain.

I mentioned the feelings of pleasure and pain. We might do well to consider these as existing on a continuum. Does doing something, or not doing it, move us more in one direction more than the other? Do we feel better by keeping a deceased loved one's belongings, or by letting them go? And then what of the relevance, benefit, or the avoidance of pain contrasted with the joys of pleasant memories? And again, we need to ask for whom are we doing it, whether *keeping items or letting them go. Of course, we cannot work this out like some algebraic problem or some detailed analysis. It would be much too complex for that. However, what we can do is to select some important aspects and then look at them with a soft focus, "reading between the lines" with introspection, listening with the heart, trusting divine guidance and the deepest yearnings of the soul. Perhaps we could use a scale from one to ten within which we would rate the pain, which may or may not reflect the deep joy or assurance we receive at the same time that it hurts. It is often remarked that happiness (or joy or love) and pain are two sides of the coin. So, since we cannot* quantify *it in terms of a formula with degrees or numbers, we can only* qualify *it—it is what it is. What we feel is what we feel, and that depends on who we are, what we are dealing with, and what we make of it emotionally and cognitively. But we might still start with a rating scale.*

So let's try asking this question: "In considering the things that I have in my possession, on a scale from 10 to 1, with 10 representing the most important, the most beneficial, or the most meaningful to me (or to others I deeply care about), and 1 representing the least beneficial, the least important, or the least meaningful to me or to the others—how would I rate the following statement for a selected item or a group of items?"

"This holds a special benefit, importance, or meaning to me, or to someone I love."

As an example, as I mentioned earlier, I have an old brass desk flip calendar that was my dad's. I'm not sure I know how old it is, but I would guess that it goes back at least 70 or 80 years. It's not something that I would have picked out or bought for myself, but knowing that it was his, and it being so unique, I chose to hold on to it. My dad kept it until the end, and therefore I assumed that it was something that he liked and perhaps appreciated its uniqueness. So,

I decided to keep it. It has meaning for me. At the other extreme, when I was going through my parents' possessions after their deaths, I needed to decide what to do with their furniture and clothes. I donated what I could to thrift shops and the remainder ended up in the trash bags. There were some interesting but broken pieces of bric-a-brac, figurines, and some inexpensive artwork which did not appeal to me at all. I'm sure my parents had kept them for a while, but I saw nothing special in them. I didn't see any marketable value in them, nor was I able to think of anyone else that might appreciate them. So, they went into the trash.

I recently decided to browse through one of my journals during the second "wake-up call" period in my life, into which I spilled my fears, sadness, struggles, and insights. Here is one passage that I wrote when cleaning out my parents' home after I had moved them to a nursing home:

"I've started to go through some of their belongings that I have begun to bring back from their home to mine. It has been difficult, though, as I'm not yet sure of how to sort and how to discern what to keep, and what to give away, and who to give things to. To be honest, it is something that I'm not looking forward to, and I hope that my delay in this is the right thing to do now. I've debated with myself and others on how to sort, store, and handle the items from their house. Since my parents have not asked about their belongings —and have very space for them anyway in their room at the facility —it is landing on me to decide how things should be handled. The one thing that makes the most sense now is to take a week between visits, taking the time to go through their things at their house, and when I am visiting them, encouraging their reflection on their belongings and in my being a good listener and a steward of their possessions."

I was sad to take on that pre-death cleaning work but knew that I needed to do it — for both them and for me.

So, in our considering objects or groups of items, we can take a "qualitative" look at the items, because of what they are and what meaning or value (or lack thereof) we can assign to them. However, in using the rating scale from 10 down to 1, we can assign point values to each one which will help us make the decisions of what to do with them, which provides us with a "quantitative" way of making our decisions for these items. Let's consider that these are our choices of what to do with our things, on the spectrum from treasures to trash:

a) to keep,

b) to share,

c) to sell,

d) to donate,

e) to recycle,

f) to toss, or

g) to take actions yet to be decided, as we are not really sure of what to do with them.

Try this: Draw out your value scale with "10" on the left side of the horizontal line, and then write out the numbers equally distant and decreasing numerically from ten down to one, with "1" on the far right, like this:

10---9---8---7---[6---5] ---4---3---2---1

You will notice that the numbers 6 and 5 have brackets around them. You might find a way of doing this that is more colorful, fun, or makes more sense to you. Either way, here is how it can work:

Begin with making and printing (you may want several copies) your "10 to 1" worksheet, with a place for the name of your item, items, or categories across the top. Select just one item or category to begin with.

Each time you decide to act on something, get out a fresh worksheet, fill in the name of the item or the category at the top, and then ask yourself these questions: 1) "What value is this to me?", and 2) "What do I want to do with this?" At this point, you would look to see how you have valued it. If you have assigned something a value between 10 and seven, decide if you want to

1) keep it,

2) share it, or gift it to someone else who would appreciate it, or

3) sell it.

If, however, you assigned a value from 4 down to 1, then you might try to determine if you want or need to

1) donate it,

2) recycle it, or

3) toss it.

What is now left then would be those items to which you would have assigned a value of 5 or 6. These would represent the things that you're not yet clear on.

So, to recap, the most important and meaningful items you would either keep, share with another, or sell for the monetary value (or make it available for another collector or a museum director who has been looking for exactly that item that you have). The least important and the least valuable or meaningful items you would then be free to either donate, recycle, or simply throw away. The ones that are right in the middle of your scale—the ones you may not know what to do with—are the ones that you would set aside or get back to later after dealing with both the highly ranked items and the lower ranked items.

There are any number of ways in which you might then sort and physically arrange or move these items. You might decide to do one drawer, one box, or one room at a time, separating the items into the named/numbered piles, boxes, or bags. You could also go through several drawers, boxes, or rooms, and then gather your items by rank, in effect putting the 10s and 9s together and working your way down to the groups of things to sell, donate, recycle, or discard in the trash. Again, the ones that you aren't sure about (the 6s and the 5s) could just be left where you found them to decide on at another time, or perhaps you might put them together in their own new pile, box, or bag, being grouped and decided on later.

> "Just do the next right thing, one thing at a time." —Glennon Doyle

As I journal, I continue to gain more clarity on this sorting strategy. Those things in our first group, being the highest rated ones, are the ones that are most meaningful, useful, joy producing, and valuable. These are the things which we keep, enjoy, use on a regular or an occasional basis, treasure, benefit through giving or sharing with others, or collect and hold onto in order to sell or to gain profit, or that we anticipate we will need at some future point. Again, these are the things that we would rate from a 10 down to a 7 on our 10 to 1 scale. For this group, there is no question that we would want to keep, use, enjoy, treasure, or add to these possessions.

The next group are those things which we know for sure we do not want, cannot use, and cannot sell. They may be broken, outdated, or too worn out, and we have no one in mind that would want the items. They have served their purpose, yet a few of them might still be a benefit to others in a shelter or a thrift shop. Other items may be kinder to the earth through their being responsibly recycled, and the remainder of the items or stuff—what we might legitimately refer to as "junk' at this point—is best relegated to the trash. Again, these are the things that we would rate four and below on our scale.

Finally, there are those things we can't decide on, so we hesitate. They are the things we would rate on the scale as a 6 or a 5. We are not immediately certain if the item is a 7 or above—where we know it has value for us—or if it rates a 4 or below and we know immediately that we do not want it. This group then, accounting for roughly 20% of our continuum, often hangs us up; we're not sure how to handle it: "does it stay or does it go?" When we apply the 80/20 rule[2], it represents the 20% of work that takes 80% of our time to process. It's not the definite yes *or the strong* no, *but the* I'm not sure *that holds us up. Accepting this allows us to plan for it, to avoid engaging in negative self-talk as we group, stack, sort, box, or toss these items.*

I am reminded of a woman who shared her remarkable story of the 3 boxes that she discovered about 2 years after a move to their new but smaller place in the country. The boxes were full, taped shut, and unmarked. After trying to remember what might be in the boxes, unable to recall anything that they had missed since their move, she and her husband took the boxes and put them into their next yard trash bonfire, unopened. They realized that if they did open them and looked inside, they would have to deal with more decisions as to what to do with the contents. While this might be a bit radical for many people, it is not an altogether bad idea to at least set aside the "I'm not sure" boxes until some time has passed.

There are a good many books and resources available for the specific mechanics of sorting and thinning. Some are both as simple and deep as asking if it elicits joy in us, while others encourage our sorting items into three, four, five, or six piles as we do the work. For specific recommendations, I am choosing to defer here to those professional organizers and authors; yet I will say this:

1) *know what you want and need to keep, share, or sell;*

2) *know what you do not want or need to keep; and*

3) *tackle the "I'm not sure" group only after dealing with the "must keep" and the "must let go of" ones.*

Some books that I have found especially helpful here include The Gentle Art of Swedish Death Cleaning[3] *(geared toward thinning positions in one's later years, both for one's own and for others' benefit);* Finding Peace, One Piece at a Time[4] *(especially supportive in the case of a spouse or a significant other's death);* Scaling Down: Living Large in a Smaller Space[5] *(with great ideas for several situations involving downsizing); and* Passed and Present *(offering many helpful and creative ideas for dealing with the deliberate care and repurposing of a loved one's items.)*[6]

In the past when I have shared these book suggestions with others, people seem to get the idea and the need for "scaling down," "downsizing," "purposeful thinning," They also get the need for learning ways to deal with a loved one's personal possessions after the other has died, and how difficult this can be. Creating a special box of small personal items and meaningful objects can be an especially meaningful way to collect and hold these items in one special place. Finding creative ways to remember others and repurpose items also usually clicks with people. Many create special scrapbooks and photo albums, and some commission works of art and remembrance ranging from jewelry containing small amounts of the deceased's "cremains" to living memorials in the form of tattoos. However, people are often mystified or unsettled whenever the term "Swedish Death Cleaning" (or "döstädning") is mentioned. Yes, it is a term unfamiliar to most all of us. According to Margareta Magnusson, who authored the book, The Gentle Art of Swedish Death Cleaning, it simply means "that you remove unnecessary things and make your home nice and orderly when you think the time is coming closer for you to leave the planet."[7] In her book, Magnusson goes on to give many examples and variations of that, along with several helpful tips, but I think you can get the picture behind the mystery of the term. Perhaps thinking in terms of "life cleaning" instead of "death cleaning" might make it a little easier to take on the work of getting rid of the unnecessary in your home.

CHAPTER 8
GETTING HELP

> *"No one who achieves success does so without acknowledging the help of others. The wise and confident acknowledge this help with gratitude."*
> —Alfred North Whitehead

Well, here I am, back in my room after my morning routine of prayer, breakfast, coffee, and a walk. My most recent journaling of "work" is very much aligned with the category, as I spent two long days and nights working on it. Today, I am focusing my reflections and this journal on the topic of help.

As I write about these processes, I am quick to remember the help that I received from others after my losses, help that I very much needed. Where did my help come from? As I look back, I would list the following categories of all those who have been gracious and beneficial to me: pastoral support from chaplains and clergy; spiritual directors; therapists; doctors; veterinarians; good friends and neighbors; cousins; funeral directors; real estate agents; bankers; elder care attorneys; hospital and nursing home staff; donation center pickups; trash collectors; self-storage managers, etc. This may not be all of them, but probably are the ones that stand out most. Again, a shared entry from my earlier journal:

"Elena, the admissions coordinator at the nursing home, was extremely good in getting them both assessed and admitted. Once she got them situated, I was able to go to the bank, the lawyer, and the real estate agent's offices for the financial and the legal issues. I got the power of attorney work in place with the facility and the bank, getting myself added to their checking and savings accounts. I headed back to the house to start assessing the situation ..."

Little did I know that in less than two months I would be adding my parents' funeral director's name and info to my contacts list, having one more person who would be invaluable in the work needed in caring for my parents.

While we are on the topic of getting help with home disbandment or downsizing, I can visualize another continuum or spectrum. At one end, you do absolutely nothing, but the "help" will be there later, working with or without you, and often at their expense—physically, emotionally, and financially. Your loved ones, children, and grandchildren will be the ones doing all the heavy physical, fiscal, and emotional lifting. As my parents' only surviving child, this is where I found myself. Most people see this as "handing down" a burden to others, rather than a gift. At the other end of the spectrum might be the decision to call a "1-800-Go Junk" type service, or to rent your own dumpster, within which you and a small army throw just about everything in it that you or your loved ones owned. And there are still others who are unable to deal with the work (with its emotional and physical challenges) and abandon their home, *responsibilities, and possessions, at times even abandoning their remaining family. Obviously, these are the extreme measures which I cannot recommend. Others will be involved whom you either pay, burden, or who will end up feeling overwhelmed, heartbroken, and angry while they are grieving. In addition to doing the "Swedish Death Cleaning" while you are still able, another great idea for making things easier for others (and letting others know of your wishes) is to consider using resources like* The Last Chapter Workbook, *which is an excellent guidebook developed by Therese McKechnie, LSCSW, to help you collect important documents and clearly record your pre- and post-death decisions.*[1] *Another excellent book is* In Case You Get Hit by a Bus: How to Organize Your Life Now for When You Are Not Around Later, *by Abby Schneiderman and Adam Seifer, the co-founders of the company Everplans. This well-written (and even fun to read) book goes into much more detail regarding the need for sharing information on the management of the home, digital accounts, passwords and password storage, etc.*[2]

We also cannot forget the help—or the hindrance—of siblings and other relatives when dealing with our parent's things. Since my siblings had died prior to the disbanding of my parents' home and their deaths, I have often shared with others that while I lamented that I didn't have my siblings to help in that difficult time, I also was grateful that I didn't have siblings to fight with over our parents' belongings! So, while I personally didn't have to share these decisions and work with siblings, I have since witnessed quite a spectrum of adult sibling support and rivalry when the second parent dies. When it is good, it's good; when it is bad, it can be really bad. Issues can include strong feelings between those who have been providing care and those who haven't, who lived nearby (or in the home) and who had long since moved far away, who has a right to this or that, and who doesn't, etc. These and many more can all surface within families. I have learned that siblings who got along as kids usually get even closer as they age, and those who fought as kids often grow more distant over the years and are more likely to fight, especially if there are nice possessions or inheritances involved. Working together is obviously ideal, and the authors whom I have already mentioned have some wonderful suggestions to help adult siblings and other relatives work together on who does what and who gets what after the fact. For this topic, I can specifically recommend the "Scaling Down" book that I have already mentioned. And of course, as Magnusson recommends in her "Swedish Death Cleaning" book, getting these things decided beforehand is best.

So, in the very middle of this spectrum in which most of us live and work and care for others is the territory of thoughtful and purposeful work in dealing with our possessions before family or others would need to do this work. These decisions and the effort needed—although they may not be easy—may in the long run be the best for all involved. What I am talking about here is responsible consuming, meaningful collecting, thoughtful gifting, and eco-friendly donating, recycling, and disposal. In taking on this important but often difficult work, who—and when—do we ask for help?

Here are some suggestions: Do your research. Plan ahead. Look at the costs. Look at the benefits. Name your friends. Develop a plan for your family and children, and work with them for their wishes as well. Be specific in your requests for help. Ask for and get referrals to professionals for the various services needed, such as eldercare or estate and tax attorneys, financial advisors, real estate agents, licensed social workers or counselors, funeral directors, senior move managers, home organizers, etc. Find and use whatever helps to keep you motivated, such as music, spiritual practices, times connecting with friends, or daily walks. "Keep your eyes on the prize" of reaching your goal. Find or create a sorting space. Hire an organizer or a senior move manager for ideas, assignments, and coaching—but not for sorting papers—and allow me the space here to tell you why.

About a dozen years ago I had hired an organizer to help me "tame the paper tiger" of my parent's belongings, and by the end of the day she had provided a lot of truly valuable help on teaching me how to organize, sort, box, store, and deal with items. After she had finished and left, I happened to look in the trash and found a $100 bill inside an envelope that she had somehow missed or overlooked. The lesson? You need to touch everything personally as you sort. This is good, in that 1) you process what you are making decisions about, perhaps doing a bit of life review of your own or for your loved ones, and 2) you never know what you might miss or end up throwing into the trash. Also—decide on and get the tools that you need, such as heavy-duty trash bags, boxes, file folders, and bold pens or a label maker. You might use motivational music, whether fast paced, instrumental, or songs from a playlist with inspirational lyrics. Consider setting smaller goals such as one dresser, one closet, one room, or even one drawer at a time. For example, in my completing the Cape Cod marathon years ago, I improved my time from my first marathon by setting and achieving 26.2 goals for the event, instead of one giant 26.2-mile effort. I broke it into these 26.2 smaller goals, one mile at a time, and with the last 252 yards as a celebratory finish for the race.

> *"Perseverance is not a long race; it is many short races one after the other."* —Walter Elliot

When we are grieving a loved one's death, others will typically offer the "whatever you need" statements. This is kind of them. However, when we are mourning and dealing with shock, we often are unable to name just what it is that we need. We are typically stunned, overwhelmed, and often numb, angry, and emotionally and physically incapable of doing anything. I think that the task of downsizing one's own or a loved one's possessions puts us in a similar place. We need the presence, support, guidance, encouragement, and the actual physical and practical help from others. And similarly, we are also often unable to state exactly what we need or how another can help us. Considerate of others, we often do not want to burden another when we are burdened. While some of us can predict or suggest specifics in the ways that others can help, it seems that the majority aren't able to do so. Recognizing and accepting this is a place to start.

"The secret of getting ahead is getting started." —Mark Twain

Whether the heavy lifting is physical or emotional, ASK! During my time of going through my parents' possessions, I found myself unable to really go through the volume of material until I asked one of my best friends to come and sit with me while I did the thinning. Like Job's friends, one of the best things others can do for us is to just show up and sit with us in our anguish and our grief—not assigning blame or giving unhelpful advice. Friends are also able to help with specific tasks or duties, as long as they know what our game plan is. I highly recommend the gift of good friends in this work, and especially those who might have different gifts or skills to contribute. However, again, I also highly recommend that you personally be the only one who touches every item and piece of paper before they are donated to strangers, shredded, or thrown away. Please don't forget my story of the $100 bill.

For things that are worth selling, auction or estate sale companies will come out and try to sell everything—except for those items that you have marked to keep—in a professionally managed estate sale. Consignment shops are one option for selling nicer things like clothing, antiques, and furniture. For the large-scale disposal and bulky trash work, companies for hire can come and take away anything that you don't want within reason, with the possible exceptions being hazardous materials. Other companies can deliver a pod to your driveway, giving you temporary sorting space at home, or for transporting your possessions to a short or long-term storage facility. And still others will deliver various sizes of dumpster units that you fill up, which they will then pick up and take away to a landfill when you request it. If you have a lot to dispose of but want to have a say as to where it might go, many communities are increasingly scheduling and holding recycling events where you can drop off bulky items, tires, paper for recycling and shredding services, electronics, clothes, furniture, home items, and even some TVs, computers, and monitors (although old CRT displays may require a co-payment to have them properly disposed of or recycled).[3]

JOURNALING GUIDE FOR PART II: FACING UP
(CHAPTERS 4–8)

1. In what ways do I hold onto or collect things that call to heart or mind "connection," "belonging," or "meaning?"

2. Look again at the list of reasons for accumulating, collecting, or holding onto possessions in chapter 4. Name those things that I have in each category that come to mind as to why I may have more stuff than I need:

    a. I never learned or was taught how to …
    b. I have too much or too little space …
    c. Waste not, want not …
    d. Survivalist … or simply stockpiling?
    e. Things that I have held onto because I am environmentally conscious, or because I remember just how much I paid for it? (For example, "I paid good money back in 1977 for that!")
    f. The major transitions of my life thus far …
    g. Having acquired others' discards or leave-behinds …

h. Sentiment, love, memories, nostalgia, and for remembering a loved one …

i. Things too painful, difficult, grief-based, or overwhelming to deal with …

j. Physical or mental inability to keep up with and physically process …

3. In naming things from the list of categories in chapter 4, name my most meaningful objects and items. Begin with "artifacts" and make entries for as many of these as I can. Next, consider in what ways these items provide me with a sense of connection, belonging, or meaning for myself, for those whom I love, my life and other relationships, and my connections with my spiritual nature, my faith, and my belief system.

Consider assigning a value from 10 down to 1 for each one and noting or deciding what to do with each item.

4. Where do I find my collecting or ownership of things to be most rewarding? What do I enjoy most in buying, collecting, or keeping? And in which ways have I found that letting go of things to be rewarding or reinforcing?

5. In considering those people, places, roles, or things that I have known or have enjoyed that I no longer have in my life—what have I kept, collected, or held on to in order to remember, appreciate, or in some way continue the relationship?

6. What objects or things do I keep in order to honor or to pay tribute to a loved one? How do I feel when looking at it or holding the item(s)? Is there a scent or fragrance that is meaningful from these items for me? Describe these feelings.

7. Consider a room, closet, drawer, or container that is "speaking" to me. Where is it? In making the decision to address it, where would I see myself starting on it? Visualize it and begin it, one room, closet, drawer, or container at a time. In what ways does using the "10 to 1" scale make it easier or more difficult for me?

8. Identify any objects or items that hold painful or heavy emotions for me or that "bring me down." What might be some ways through which I can ceremoniously let go of them? Perhaps having friends present, holding a "funeral" ritual for the objects, and having the friends afterwards take the items away?

9. Either through visualizing or physically visiting, list these areas of "home" in the order of what nags at me the most: bathroom(s), bedroom(s), closet(s), dining or eating area(s), garage, kitchen, living room or family area(s), porch and/or patio or deck, and storage areas such as basement, attic, sections of the garage, etc.

Seeing these areas, what uses up the most "attention units" for me? Which will have the most payoff by tackling first? List these in order of importance or by ease of accomplishment. Should I handle the small ones first, or the most important or pressing ones? Using the list, circle or number them in order of handling, and consider putting a date on which each will be started and completed.

10. Using my new added title of "HR Director," make a list of all those by name, skill, or a professional title whom I will seek and engage in helping me. Friends? Family? Paid professionals? It may be helpful to start with an A-Z listing, as in attorney,

banker, my BFF, my brother Bill, cousin Claire, etc., all the way through the alphabet to senior move managers, trash removers, wrecking companies, and even zookeepers if needed.

For each person, resource, or profession, assign the intended needs or tasks, the contact-by date, the dates that they have been contacted to help, and any general or specific agreements.

PART THREE
STEPPING UP

CHAPTER 9
SELF CARE OF BODY, MIND, AND SOUL

"Give yourself a gift of five minutes of contemplation
in awe of everything you see around you.
Go outside and turn your attention to the many miracles
around you. This five-minute-a-day regimen
of appreciation and gratitude will help you
to focus your life in awe."
—Wayne Dyer

This morning a light rain is falling, so after my morning prayers and breakfast I have opened the window to allow the sounds and scents of this early September morning to connect me with nature, today being the eleventh day of my working retreat. Sometimes I am so engrossed in projects, service, ministry, etc., that my own self-care gets pushed further down the list of priorities. I still need to remember to remind myself to take that time for my own needs.

Dealing with our own or another's possessions is hard work. The world is fast-paced, and both welcomed and unwelcomed interrup-

tions break up our day, affecting our work, our personal activities, and even our sleep. Breaking news, advertisements, and other things constantly break into our personal life and time. Whether you see yourself as a monk or a new monastic, finding and taking dedicated and observed times for rest, solitude, prayer or meditation, and playful activity or exercise is both absolutely necessary and extremely difficult. Eating healthfully can even be difficult. Spiritually, the origins of all major religions and their precepts record the examples and state the importance of our self-care of body, mind, and soul. Long before the now widely used idiom of "putting on your own oxygen mask first before assisting the person next to you" came into our common vernacular, our institutions of faith stressed the importance of self-care. Our creator—whether recognized or named as God, Allah, Infinite Intelligence, or the Ground of All Being (or however we each individually conceive of the foundation or the highest level of the unseen order of things)—knows that we need these things.

> "Self-love has very little to do with how you feel about your outer self. It's about accepting all of yourself." —Tyra Banks

Abraham Maslow, the great twentieth-century psychologist and founder of transpersonal psychology (psychology open to realms and concepts outside of traditional psychology, such as spirituality and transcendence), became most well-known for his hierarchy of needs that postulated that as our most basic and crucial physical needs for life, safety, shelter, food and water, etc., are met, we find that we have higher level needs and wants that are motivators for us. Beyond the basic needs for survival and safety are the needs for love, belonging, and esteem. Together, Maslow saw these as our "deficit" needs. As we are able to meet our deficit needs, we are free to focus on what Maslow termed our "being" needs, those needs for self-fulfillment in growth, the search and enjoyment of beauty, directed toward accomplishment, learning, greater knowledge, etc. Having many of these met, in Maslow's view, allowed an individual to aspire to reach higher—in accomplishments, learning, and creative pursuits—and growing and developing to the highest level one is capable of.[1] Later in his life, Maslow saw a penultimate human growth need beyond self-actualization, which he and others have also described as either a level of "transcendence" or "selfless actualization," with a moving beyond self to traverse cosmic, ego, body, and social realms.

These needs are organic, evolving and growing; hierarchical, yet not invariant. Things change, and our needs change. Meeting a lower level or basic need does not mean that the need isn't still constantly there. Someone who feels safe with a secure home and happy marriage but then tragically loses one or both due to a fire, violence, or a catastrophic storm would find themselves struggling to regain their footing at the most basic level. In contrast, there are those few who, despite their not having the basics needed for a decent life, are somehow able to transcend their circumstances. While homeless, hungry, and living in disadvantaged or even war zone circumstances, some do find and meet the higher-level needs—and not just for themselves, but also for others. Movement in Maslow's model, then, isn't just continual progressive movement up the pyramid, but in an upward, downward, both/and flow of dynamic, organic movement.

The new higher-level needs, in both one's awareness and attainment, once realized and achieved—or even perhaps just glimpsed and tasted—are not easily forgotten or abandoned. Like the saying that a mind, once expanded, never returns to its original size, we are designed to seek higher goals after the basic and the mid-level needs are satisfied. Maslow's work was done in the framework of motivation, yet he and others since saw within the model the aspirational growth potential from which the human growth potential movement, and later the field of Positive Psychology, grew.

So: Where does this all fit with the work of managing one's—or another's—possessions?

Those who write about and coach others on organization and clutter control, as in the Clutter's Last Stand *books,[2] stress the importance of controlling what you have, and not being controlled or ruled by it. While we know—as does the Infinite Source of all Being, that we need things to live—there is a point of excess. Clutter overcomes the clean, disorder subsumes the order, and overactivity takes all the energy or the oxygen out of the room, with little left for the space that is needed for the peace, the precious, or the spiritual. David Steindl-Rast, OSB, in his book,* The Music of Solitude, *states that we need the space between the notes in music.[3] Likewise, we need to find or make room in our lives to allow the beauty of our song to arise and live. Let us remember Mr. Spock's words, "Live long and prosper." When we wish another a long life,[4] we are not just talking about physical longevity, but also about prospering across many realms, whether they be relationships, material security, or our internal resources of heart, mind, and soul. We prosper to the degree that we can meet not only our "deficit" needs, but our "be-ing" needs. We prosper with the strength of our positive, healthy, and loving relationships.*

> "Do not give your heart to that which does not satisfy your heart."
> —Abba Poemen

The great contemplative Fr. Thomas Keating envisioned what he referred to as the "welcoming prayer" and the "emotional programs for happiness," as helpfully explained by Cynthia Bourgealt in her book, Centering Prayer and Inner Awakening.*[5] I was introduced to this a couple of years ago by Sr. Margaret, for which I am forever grateful. Using an inverted triangle diagram, the three interrelated and different—yet equal—unconscious emotional program needs are labeled as power/control, esteem/affection, and security/survival. When these are threatened, our happiness and our relationships can be turned upside down. Conflicts can then erupt within ourselves and with others when our programs (or schema) for happiness are threatened. The path to avoiding these conflicts is to embrace and practice the art of welcoming and then letting go of those desires—our desires for control, affection, and security.*

So, if we are truly able to glimpse into our subconscious or unconscious needs for these three pairings of Keating's emotional programs for happiness, we might better come to see and appreciate —and even own—our needs, both met and unmet. We may consider this to be yet another continuum. This continuum may be viewed as one of contrasting contentment vs. conflict, assurance of inner peace vs. the threats of disruption, or personal empowerment vs. impotency. The more we are aware of things that inspire, motivate, and evoke happiness—as well as those that dishearten, threaten, or sadden us—the better we can move in the direction of greater inner peace and a healthier mind, body, and soul. As in the oxygen mask metaphor I shared earlier, our good self-care in all these realms can then extend outward to all others for relational and communal harmony.

While this is not in any way a treatise on mindfulness, what I am trying to convey here certainly references and encourages these intentions and practices. Once considered as existing only in Eastern religions and philosophies such as Zen Buddhism, or as part of the "New Age" movement, these practices have now been studied, recognized, and widely accepted and promoted in the fields of Western medicine and mental health. In fact, many mindfulness therapies and practices have now met the standards to be considered "evidence-based" and legitimate. In our exploring the importance of self-care in our management of our possessions, these too have a place here. In our doing this hard work in a fast-paced world—the need to slow down, become centered or grounded, and to be mindful—cannot be overstressed.

"What exactly is mindfulness?" you might ask. Jon Kabat-Zinn, the author of Wherever You Go, There You Are,[6] *and long recognized as a leader in the mindfulness movement, defines it this way: "Mindfulness means paying attention in a particular way: on purpose, in the present moment, and nonjudgmentally." After both studying and practicing mindfulness, I am convinced that it not only helps us feel more centered, but it also helps us physically (somatically), mentally, and emotionally. It even improves our productivity. While it is not exactly meditation, mindfulness certainly shares a lot with meditation and contemplative prayer. We slow down and become more aware of who and where we are and how we feel.*

> *"The ability to be in the present moment is a major component of mental wellness."* —Abraham Maslow

In being more mindful, we become more aware of our surroundings, along with the multitude of the smaller things and even those miracles that we miss or take for granted.

My belief also is that not only can mindfulness center us in the present, but it can also help us expand time. Let me explain.

First, let's consider the metaphor, "X marks the spot"—the symbol on the map that tells us exactly where a treasure is buried. At some point later I came to learn that we also can use the "X" to identify our location in our life.

I began to use this in my sessions and groups with others, stating that the intersection of two diagonal lines, the X, represents where we are at this moment. What is below the X is our past or former life; what is above it is our future, our self-to-be. When I finish drawing and explain the diagram and concept, I draw two new diagonal lines over the first X, with the lines just a shade higher than the old ones.

Here, I explain, is where we are at this very moment, this new moment. This new now. This is the present moment that Kabat-Zinn wrote of, and each new moment is the new now, the present. The X spot has moved forward, as have we. Have we been present, or aware, in this present moment? Seriously—have we? Then I point out—as Eckhart Tolle did in The Power of Now—*that we live neither in the past nor in the future. We only live in the present.*[7] *Each new moment is our present. The less mindful we are, the less we really live in the present. We may continue to exist, but to paraphrase that old advertising slogan, "better living through chemistry," there is "better living through mindfulness."*

> *"Life can be found only in the present moment. The past is gone, the future is not yet here, and if we do not go back to ourselves in the present moment, we cannot be in touch with life."* —Thich Nhat Hanh

And so, in my opinion, here is where it gets really interesting: *When we are less aware in the present, the present slips by. Perhaps we are being mindless as we carry out the tasks of the day while multitasking, or by passively watching media content on our devices. Have you ever noticed that? Perhaps we are spending our present moment by living in the past through nostalgia and longing, or through ruminating, shame, doubt, guilt, unforgiveness, etc., or conversely, in effect spending our life trying to live into the future through obsessive planning or worrying. However, by practicing mindfulness, we can, in effect,* expand *the present moment, that center of the X.*

In our being mindful, we are widening the time we have in the present with the now, which is the only place where we actually live. *Why not then take full advantage of the present, for each moment that we are given?*

Here are some helpful techniques you can employ to develop your mindfulness:

On her website, the noted retreat leader and author Tara Brach freely shares her meditation practice. She named it RAIN, and suggests using it as a guide for mindfulness and becoming present. Here is how she defines it:

"The acronym RAIN is an easy-to-remember tool for bringing mindfulness and compassion to emotional difficulty.

- ***R****ecognize what is going on;*
- ***A****llow the experience to be there, just as it is;*
- ***I****nvestigate with interest and care;*
- ***N****urture with self-compassion."*

The RAIN meditation, along with relaxed and focused breathing, can be a wonderful tool that you can do in less than 15-20 minutes. It helps during meditation to pay attention to your body in what is called a "body scan," where you check in or get in touch with which parts of your body are relaxed, tense, uncomfortable, etc.

Another good tool for helping ground yourself, lower your stress level, and place yourself in a position of more mindfulness is to use the popular "5-4-3-2-1" practice, referenced on many websites. Basically, it involves ...

5: Acknowledge FIVE things you see around you ...
4: Acknowledge FOUR things you can touch around you ...
3: Acknowledge THREE things you hear ...
2: Acknowledge TWO things you can smell ...
1: Acknowledge ONE thing you can taste ... and then follow with a deep breath.

(Personally, unless I am eating at that moment or have something to drink like a warm cup of coffee or tea nearby, I acknowledge the items 5, 4, 3, and 2, and leave off the acknowledgment of taste).

I recommend trying at least one of these, and practice it as you do your hard work of purposeful possessions management. Be conscious and open toward being centered and grounded. Practicing these will help as you do the work of processing your feelings and emotions of grief and deep gratitude, in your remembering, your prioritizing, and in your hope.

CHAPTER 10
THE PATH OF HEALING AND GROWTH

*"Growth is uncomfortable;
you have to embrace the discomfort
if you want to expand."*
—Jonathan Majors

Well, after two more longer-than-expected days spent exploring and journaling on self-care, we are now moving forward toward coalescing all that I have written thus far. I have already devoted part of this Sunday morning to morning prayers and a light breakfast outside, and after my walk I settled back in my room for reflection and writing time. Today's mission is to pull things together so that we can move ahead.

"OK," you might say to yourself, "I now can see how and why my closets, my home, my trunk, and my life, have become so full and unmanageable. I can now better grasp the motivations for collecting and possessing, and the ways we define or describe what we own. I *can identify with how change equals loss equals grief, and the influence of grief on collecting and keeping. I can also see now how some intentional collecting and saving helps me process my grief. You provided me with some great insight and a few practical ways to address more healthy and efficient possessions management, and when and who and how to ask for help. Now, you have just shared the importance of self-care for body, mind, and soul, along with the value of mindfulness and some practical ways to become more mindful. You have definitely helped me to see the importance of living in the present. So, now what? Since I very much want to be less encumbered and less controlled by my possessions, to have a clean and usable "trunk," and to use less of my "attention units"[1] when I get in my car or when I walk by a closet—how do I create a new path? How do I blaze a new trail through the forest toward greater mental and emotional freedom and a more calming sense of inner peace? How do I create that space in my life for who and what is in it that is meaningful to me? How do I begin? How do I energize my motivation for implementing positive change? What can I hope to achieve, physically, mentally, emotionally, spiritually, and relationally? And how can I grow through my grief as I do this?"*

Well, let's start with a short refresher that we learned in school years ago. The prefix "re" can be considered a "morpheme", an interesting tool in the English language. A morpheme, as you may or may not recall from high school grammar, is the smallest unit of sound, which when combined with different words produces new meanings. I first really became aware of this from something the author/educator Parker Palmer wrote: that the word "remember" can be seen as the need to connect with that part of us which is no longer present or attached, in effect, to re-member what or whom we no longer have with us. I have had so many people say to me that in losing a loved one they felt like they had lost a part of themselves; some even reporting feeling as if they had lost their right arm. Whether a loved one, a friend, or a team of co-workers—when someone goes away or is taken away, by a job change, a move, natural death, an accident or by violence—we remember them in order to re-member, reattach, or keep them connected to our body or group. So, here I will use the "re" morpheme to stress again those main reasons why we possess, collect, and hold on to things, as well as our memories: Connection. Belonging. Meaning.

Here are several "re" words and some suggestions that can help in this process of reclaiming your life's space: revisit, review, resolve, refuse, refocus, reduce, recommit, renew, reinvest, and rededicate.

1. **Review and revisit** *your life, through life reviews at various points or milestones in your life, and take a good look at your habits, your thoughts, self-talk (positive or negative), etc. Take a good look at how you think, how and what you feel, what your perceptions and emotions are, and any reactions in your behavior, in both the helpful and the unhelpful habits and traditions that you have acquired along the way.*
2. **Resolve** *to do it now. "Do it now!" This phrase has been stated in so many ways by so many philosophers and organizational experts over the centuries—yet it cannot be overstated. Start today, even on something small.*
3. **Refuse** *to cling to or be controlled by clutter or possessions. Refuse to cling to things of the past that are not helpful for you either now or in the future.*
4. **Refocus** *on what and who is important and meaningful in your life. Again, I'm not suggesting that all things be thinned, but only those things which do not have special meaning or serve a purpose for you and others in your life. In your resolve to move forward, let go of those things that*

distract and deter you from the positive and the purposeful in your life.

5. **Reduce** *the number of things which do not serve some good purpose for you, and rediscover the good and the important things that you have lost or misplaced which often lie beneath, covered up by the less important things.*

6. **Recommit** *to living a more uncluttered life. Another popular idiom (although one typically not well practiced) is that of "Less is more," stressing the order and the psychological as well as the spiritual freedom that comes from practicing simplicity. I think this is felt when we go on vacation or retreat to an uncluttered and clean hotel room, a guest house, a room at a convent or monastery, or a rental home. In her book,* The Gentle Art of Swedish Death Cleaning, *author Margareta Magnusson suggests many benefits from going through your possessions while still of sound mind and body. In addition to being able to process your life as you sort—reliving joys and sadness, recalling lessons and gratitude, etc.,—you are not only able to provide joy to others through meaningful gifts, but you can enjoy simplicity and cleaner living space as you do!*

7. **Renew and reinvest** *in your present life as you are now living it, with a nod to the past and a hopeful look to the future. To name what you have lost and what you have gained can be a starting point of wisdom. To let go of that which is no longer helpful or needed so that you may be open to new blessings, both those hidden under the clutter in your life and those which are yet to be realized. To live this new life, with fewer distractions, is to help free up your attention units. And to reincorporate healthy and helpful habits which you know or suspect will be good for you— following a good diet and your physician's orders, quality*

> *movement or exercising, taking in the benefits of the outdoors, prayer or meditation, journaling, reading, socializing and sharing with good friends and loved ones, listening to good music, dancing, walking, and so on.*
> 8. ***Rededicating*** *yourself to the memories of those whom you love but see no longer through intentionally honoring and paying tribute to them in ways that are personal for you and them. Perhaps publicly rededicating your life in helping others as a way of honoring a loved one. Taking "commemorative" travel trips as a personal pilgrimage for reconnecting—both with yourself and with others. It's worth exploring. An example would be a trip to a special place you and a loved one enjoyed visiting, or to a place you had hoped to visit. I have a friend who has done just that in the few years since her husband died, with trips to Katmandu, India, and Peru.*

As a good part of my writing involves working through grief, what is being suggested here actually fits nicely with the work of William Worden, PhD, who identified four necessary tasks that we ideally move through as we work through our grief.[2] I suggest using the acronym TEAR to serve as a reminder of the four tasks.

Here they are in my paraphrasing:

1. ***T****otally accept the reality of the loss*
2. ***E****xperience the pain of the loss*
3. ***A****djust to life without the person or your life as it had been*
4. ***R****einvest in this new life, reconnecting with others as you move forward through grief*

Moving forward through loss or through the transitions of life involves change, and since significant change can elicit emotions of grief, Dr. Worden's tasks are very much worth including here in our discussion of healing and growth, from possessing much, to keeping only the best and most meaningful. One of the saddest stories from my time working with hospice patients and their families had to do not with the patient's impending death and her family's grief, but instead her lost opportunity to do a life review and to be able to go through and reflect on and distribute her possessions. Like many, she and her husband had been aging in place for some time. When she was placed on hospice care and a move to a care center was necessary, the move happened quickly, without her being able to sort through her things and do her pre-death cleaning. She had waited too long. When she was provided the opportunity for the gift of a special day to have and do anything she wanted, her wish was to go back to the home and go through her stuff. By this time, however, her condition had worsened to the point where it was no longer possible. She died without being able to do what she had really desired to do for her own and her family's benefit. So please, do not let this happen to you.

CHAPTER II
SIMPLICITY

> *"Simplicity is making the journey of this life with just baggage enough."*
> —*Charles* Dudley Warner

Well, after the two days I needed to delve properly into the last chapter, the importance of simplicity began to come more into my consciousness. Since I am focusing on simplicity, I will make it the shortest chapter—"less is more," after all. Will I succeed? Perhaps, and perhaps not. I think that—other than some sort of forced or accidental simplicity—simplicity is not simple. So again, after my morning routine, I am now back at the desk as I reflect and write ...

"Less is more." It sounds like an oxymoron, doesn't it? How, exactly, can less be more? Think back to what I wrote earlier about mindfulness. From Julian of Norwich's profound insight of seeing all of creation in something the size of a hazelnut, and from what we are learning of quantum physics and spirituality, things at the very core *may actually be both dense and expansive. Some believe that the universe, all of creation, is present at the very smallest level. I must confess that I really have no good idea of how this is, and certainly would be foolish to try to discuss it any further. I will admit that I am clearly out of my league here. So, short of trying to describe the collapsing or expansion of all matter and energy into the densest level possible or trying to theorize about the nature of "black holes," let's just look at our own lives, however simple or complex they may be.*

While we enjoy so many things that make our lives better than our ancestors', we certainly have more issues to deal with now—access to information, access to healthcare, affordability, the need to learn and juggle any number of new technologies. For those of us who grew up in the early 1960s, we might still remember the performances of Erich Brenn on the Ed Sullivan show,[1] whose skill was spinning plates on poles. He and the audience weren't satisfied with his spinning just one or two plates. No, he had so many spinning at one time from so many poles that we would all marvel at the plates seemingly defying gravity (or, as kids, just waiting to see if they would fall and crash!). For many of us, life often feels like we have too many plates spinning. Using another plate metaphor, we sometimes tell others that our plate is so full that we cannot take on one more thing. We might also consider the metaphor of "Groundhog Day" from the eponymous film,[2] where our protagonist keeps repeating the same day. Or quite possibly the metaphor of being stuck on a merry-go-round strikes a chord with you.

Perhaps we could describe our situation as a state of saturation. Like a sponge that has soaked up all that it can hold, we cannot take on or hold anything more. A cup of tea that is full to the brim cannot contain any more. We long for time off, for vacation, for 5:00 PM to roll around, or for the weekend. Our lives are music, and we need more space between the notes to avoid experiencing either a cacophony or a drone. We need time and space for our souls to catch up with our bodies. The early ascetics retreated to the desert to live as hermits in the early centuries of the Common Era. And in the 1800s, Ralph Waldo Emerson and Henry David Thoreau, early influencers in the naturalist and transcendental and human potential movements, retreated to the woods for solitude. They all saw the need for retreat. And these times were, of course, long before the internet, 24/7 channels and streaming services, social media, and our ability to carry instantaneous access to the world everywhere through a smartphone. Now it is nearly impossible to escape the complex and frenetic world and find a bit of simplicity and some solitude away from the noise.

Space between the notes, as in music, provides the rest, order, and the time for appreciation that we need in our lives. Like the beating of our hearts, the place of rest is what makes the next life-sustaining movement of our hearts possible.

As we learn to forgive one another and to let go of negative self-talk and emotional baggage, we come to see that these actions free us. They open the doors of the emotional prisons that we often find ourselves in, opening us to live a lighter life. Carrying around the heavy gunnysack of emotional baggage wears us down. Lightening the load opens us up to living life and working with others with our minds and our hearts unburdened. And so it is also with our possessions ...

> "Truth is ever to be found in simplicity, and not in the multiplicity and confusion of things." —Sir Isaac Newton

> "What a circus act we women perform every day of our lives. Look at us. We run a tightrope daily, balancing a pile of books on the head. Baby-carriage, parasol, kitchen chair, still under control. Steady now! This is not the life of simplicity but the life of multi-

plicity that the wise men warn us of." —Anne Morrow Lindbergh

Sitting here in my minimally—yet adequately—furnished "cell" at the guest house, I am reminded of the cartoon by the New Yorker cartoonist Charles Barsotti[3] that features a dog looking out from its small doghouse, seeing a bowl of water, a bone, and a toy, with the caption balloon reading "I have everything." Here, in my solitary place, I have been busy, and while often writing 1,300 to 1,500 words or more per day, I can say that this has been a good time for me. Time away from our normal busy lives typically serves as a respite, even if we are hard at work on something that is meaningful or important. We often experience a state of what is referred to as "flow" or as "being in the zone" during these experiences. This often brings a feeling of happiness. Earl Nightingale, a popular motivational author and speaker for many years, shared in his 1956 sound recording, "The Greatest Secret," this statement about success: "Success is the progressive realization of a worthy goal or ideal." I would suggest that his words can be applied to happiness as well: "Happiness is the progressive realization of a worthy goal or ideal." We are happiest when we are working on worthy goals aligned with our core values— when we attain some measure of success—or goal achievement. For you this may be in your career, in raising healthy children, working on peace and justice issues, building a business, in growing your church, or in any callings of worthy goals or ideals.

> "Happiness is neither virtue nor pleasure nor this thing nor that but simply growth. We are happy when we are growing."
> —William Butler Yeats

Does simplicity guarantee happiness? Certainly not. It can, however, create the space and the fertile ground for it to take root. When I look back at my earlier journals from the times I was on vacation in the lush Missouri Ozarks or in the beautifully arid landscapes of the great Southwest, I can see how I most often found great peace and a fullness of depth in those get-aways, surrounded by the extraordinary beauty of the Mark Twain National Forest in Missouri, the Sonoran Desert of Arizona, or the Sangre de Cristo Mountains in New Mexico. Much of my happiness—and success—has come through those times; not just found in the incredible locations themselves, but as a result of the time away and the space to think, feel, reflect, hope, and dream. The crafting of my first personal rule of life, the subsequent revisions and renewals, and the goal setting and life planning work done in those times of vacation and retreat (like this one) have been crucial to my own progressive realization of "worthy goals and ideals."

When we are fortunate enough to be able to find a place of quiet, comfort, simplicity, and surroundings—freed from whatever constitutes work for us and the quieting of the "monkey mind" and the steeling of the physical "busybody"—like in the space between our own heartbeats, we can take the time to empty ourselves of the oppressive "have to" and "should do" statements. We can emerge replenished and reinvigorated—with new ideas, gratitude, aspirations, and goals—as our hearts are refilled, continually recirculating our blood. We can be renewed and replenished, appreciative of this moment, and open to the next.

One of my favorite verses from the Hebrew scriptures is this line from Psalm 46: "Be still and know that I am God."[4] It begins with the derivation of the Hebrew word Rapha, *meaning surrender, weakness, and letting go. Like Paul McCartney's song "Let it Be" that he wrote when struggling with The Beatles' disbandment,[5] it is about loosening our grip, relaxing, and releasing. Many consider Psalm 46:10 as perhaps the most comprehensive and perfect scripture, in that even as you take away the words from the end, it remains brilliantly instructive, as we see in it, "Be still and know that I AM . . ."*

and then becoming distilled down to the words "Be still," and finally "Be."

So how can we create or find more simplicity in our lives? While you may be thinking that I have departed from the matter of possessions, I really haven't. Here is why: We absolutely have the potential to create that place of simplicity in our own lives. And even if we cannot create it overall in our very busy lives and our often-challenging living environments, we can always find that one place, physically or meditatively, where we can withdraw and take a moment. Thus, the importance of the goal and the work of cleaning out one corner, or one room first. Instead of the well-intentioned effort to try to multitask and clean out "a little bit here, a little bit there," or perhaps more like the debt-reduction plan recommendation of paying off either the smallest debt or the highest interest credit card first, we are in fact better served to finish one thing first: one drawer, one closet, one corner of the room.

> "The more I want to get something done, the less I call it work."
> —Richard Bach

It has been said somewhere that "one book read is better than three books started." So, go ahead — find and clean at least one space at a minimum for your solitude and simplicity. Do you have something like that hanging over your head right now that might be holding you back from a sense of serenity and order, or has been increasing your sense of stress, depression, or anxiety? Why not tackle it right now? Go ahead—straighten up one drawer, clean off your coffee table, or wash those dirty dishes in the sink—and then come back to this page when you have done that one thing.

Did you get that one thing done? Or maybe two things? How did it feel? Perhaps not so great in doing it—but in having it done, you might just experience that sense of satisfaction and a bit more control over your life.

When we purposefully shed our possessions, what might be some benefits of the resulting simplicity? Here are a few: To find things more quickly. To feel less encumbered. To have the time and space to look at, touch, hear, smell, and even taste those things that bring us joy. To be reminded of another's essence without being overcome by their volume of stuff or triggered by unpleasant feelings or memories. To be inspired and informed, but not inundated. To be freed from the trash, so you can enjoy the treasures. To focus on who and what is most important and meaningful in your life. To remove the "junk" in order to better see the "jewels." To have room in your life and world to accept new blessings when they arrive. To have more room in your "attention bank" to be present to God, to the beauty in nature and creation. To be with a loved one or friend, to be able to experience a moment of just being present. To feel safe, even for one moment—this one. To build up a reserve of your units of attention so that they are available when needed for the most important things and people in your life.

As you make progress in your own purposeful shedding or thinning, and as you begin to feel some "progressive realization" of your own worthy goals or ideals, you may start to gain some initial glimpses of satisfaction through this newfound simplicity. And even if you are not able to simplify most of your world, you may be able to simplify enough of a corner of a room to sustain you or motivate you to go after more, in your own "less is more" paradigm.

The takeaway here is that few of us will ever be called to live the life of an aesthetic hermit. But we can come to realize that less really can be more, in a way that is personal to us. Progressing towards simplicity—or some may say minimalism—may even make a bit more room for the transcendent in our lives!

JOURNALING GUIDE FOR PART III: STEPPING UP
CHAPTERS 9–11

1. Before beginning this section, go back to the start of Chapter 9 and reread—and then follow—the recommendation by Dr. Wayne Dyer. Take five minutes to look around with awe and appreciation of the many miracles all around.

2. Self-love is different than self-esteem. Self-esteem speaks of judgment; self-love caresses with permission to be me, and to accept myself—all of me. Reflect on those things that are typically included in self-care, such as good diet, stress management, restorative sleep, purposeful and healthy movement, benefiting from good relationships, etc. Good self-care translates to self-love. What are some ways in which I can care for—and love—myself more?

3. Draw a triangle—one side of a pyramid—layer it in four horizontal sections, and label these from the bottom levels to the top as such:

- Level 1 (at the bottom): basic needs, such as safety and survival
- Level 2 (next up): psychological needs, such as love and belonging
- Level 3 (next up): self-fulfillment needs, such as growth and meaning
- Level 4 (very top point): transcendence, those goals outside or above oneself

While I may move up and down in this triangle, am I meeting needs at each level on a daily—or at least a regular—basis? If not, consider some ways in which I can realize and meet more of my psychological and self-fulfillment needs. When are those times in which I can care for myself as I can care for others?

4. Have I been giving myself permission to do those things that support and nourish me? Reflect on those opportunities when I can say "yes" to self, "yes" to self-care, and when it's OK to say "no" to other requests or demands.

5. Make a resolution—and a plan—to participate in those things that my body needs and enjoys, such as eating healthy and tasty nutritious food; staying active, with muscle movement for fitness and enjoyment as I am able; spending some time outdoors in nature; benefiting from restorative sleep; connecting with others; taking advantage of opportunities for giving back and sharing, etc.

6. Find and take the time for some solitude and silence in my life. Begin to practice being more present with the concept of mindfulness. Remember the "X" of living in the present. Remember to use Tara Brach's "R-A-I-N" meditation and the grounding meditation of "5-4-3-2-1" as gifts to myself.

7. Look back to the first page of chapter 10. Now complete the following sentences:

> I can now see how my ... have become so ...
> I am better able to grasp just how my losses of ... have influenced my buying, collecting, and retaining of ...
> Keeping my ... helps me by ...
> Letting go of ... helps me by ...

8. Here are some ways in which I can reclaim my life's space and move ahead on the path of healing and growth:

- Revisit and review my life
- Resolve to "do it now"
- Refuse to be controlled by clutter
- Refocus on who and what are important to me
- Reduce the less helpful and unimportant things
- Recommit to a less cluttered life, transforming "death cleaning" into "life cleaning"
- Review and reinvest in the here and now, with a more balanced and healthy life
- Rededicate and find ways to honor and pay tribute to those I love

9. Regarding my life, which of these metaphors most strike home for me? Why?

> "Spinning plates"
> "My plate is too full"
> "Merry-go-round"
> "Groundhog Day"
> "Saturated sponge"
> "Hamster wheel"

10. What are some healthy ways in which I have dealt with chaos or a lack of simplicity in my life?

11. How have my possessions controlled me and interfered with the progressive realization of my worthy goals or ideals?

12. What is something that I could do today or this week to find some simplicity, space, or solitude in my life?

13. Thinking about retreats—when did I last get away for a relaxing vacation or a replenishing retreat? Journal what that was like.

14. Can I arrange a retreat similar to a special one that I went on before? If a retreat of a few days or a week is not possible, how and where can I take "mini retreats"—to a quiet place, coffee shop, somewhere in nature, a museum, or a sacred space? List some places where I can take a mini retreat, and resolve to take or continue to take these: …

15. Imagine or visualize some ways in which freeing up possessions would provide me with more simplicity. What does that feel like? List the first three ways that come to mind. Now, pick one and go do it, and then return to write about what that was like.

PART FOUR
LIGHTENING UP

CHAPTER 12
GROWTH THROUGH LETTING GO

> *"Loss provides an opportunity to take inventory of our lives, to reconsider priorities, and to determine new directions."*
> —Gerald L. Sittser

I have been writing for over two weeks now, having gone through three ink pens and am now well into my second large notebook. Rachel and I were able to chat on the phone a bit last night, and she assured me that she had been enjoying having JoAnna there for an extended visit. In my having "sequestered" myself in the guest quarters at St. Cecilia's, I have truly realized the importance of the much-needed restorative time I've been blessed with by being here. These blessings have included the simple and pleasant lodging, food, water (and yes, wine), silence, the walks, and solace in nature, the structure and inspiration of daily prayers and each evening's Compline prayer,[1] the knowing that I am loved, the wonderful gift of Sister Margaret's spiritual companioning, and the internet—both for research and for streaming Gregorian chants. Like Barsotti's dog, I have all that I need right now.

As I look back over the past sixteen days since I arrived, I can see how much I have deeply explored. Perhaps some things have come into greater focus for those reading this, as they have for me. Recalling Captain Kirk's famous opening line on the original Star Trek series —"Space... the final frontier"—we might say: "Retrace... the way you got here," or even "Grace... the blessings of the here." To know where you came from. The past is not to be lived in, but neither is it to be forgotten. Forgiveness, however, is different. While we know that forgiveness ideally involves both the one offended and the offender—with apologies, repentance, reconciliation, and an effort for restoration—it is, in the end, typically the one doing the forgiving who benefits most. We release the anger and pain in ourselves by forgiving. We are not condoning; we are simply releasing. We are to learn from the past, so as not to relive it—as if we could—and then forgive so that we do not continue to carry that pain. Outside of deeply traumatic and painful events of the past— which ideally might be explored with the skillful help of a caring and competent professional—we can review, revisit, and even recapture the especially meaningful and instructive things, people, and experiences or events of the past, even if they are difficult and painful. I believe it was Benjamin Franklin who said, "That which hurts, also instructs." If you fall, or are pushed down, then pick something up as you get up. Painful experiences shouldn't be left there; the pain should not be wasted.

> "When you shine from various angles, you shine not because you're perfectly whole but broken, and it's how you transcend from that brokenness that sets you apart and makes you an extraordinary human being." —Danny Castillones Sillada

As we look back to remember the good times and people in our lives, we can also look back to learn—and grow stronger—from the bad times and the painfully difficult times.

In his book, A Farewell to Arms, *Ernest Hemingway wrote this: "The world breaks everyone and afterward many are stronger at the broken places."[2] In the book of Genesis in the Hebrew scriptures, we read of Jacob's wounding which was incurred from his wrestling with God. From that, his hip was dislocated, and although from that point thereafter he walked with a limp, he walked away blessed.[3] When we are experiencing pain in the now, we may find some balance through recalling the joy and happiness of the past. We may accept—and give ourselves—grace: offering and accepting our own forgiveness. We may experience some growth and blessings through the hardships. In the Japanese culture, the art of Kintsugi takes this even further: when pottery has been broken, it is repaired using lacquers combined with silver, platinum, or gold powder so as not to hide the repairs but to accentuate them. The history of the items is made visible and then considered even more beautiful.*

> "Transformation is a process, and as life happens there are tons of ups and downs. It's a journey of discovery—there are moments on mountaintops and moments in deep valleys of despair." —Rick Warren

With the grief that we have had—or continue to hold—we can find grace in the growth that has either occurred or which is possible. There is a trend in the mental health field of using the qualifier "trauma informed" when describing certain techniques or therapies. What this means is that the therapist makes sure they are aware of any trauma in the client's history and fully takes it into consideration in their treatment or intervention. It has finally come to be recognized as critically important that a healthcare provider or educator become aware of their patient's, client's, or student's traumatic history. Likewise, in grief work, there are schools of thought focusing on the possibility of a griever's growing through grief, or even their experiencing some level of "transformative grief." In transformative grief, the griever comes out not only as a changed person, but often as a better person. They have "become stronger in the broken places." They may have been wounded, but perhaps can move ahead with a new life and a new strength.

So again, whenever you fall, or are dropped or pushed to a low place, look around, and pick something up as you get back on your feet. Learn from it, grow from it. Grieve, yes, but also grow.

"So again, how are my possessions a part of this?" you might be asking. In my earlier writing on grief, in which I shared the simple equation, "Change = loss = grief," I mentioned William Worden's "Four tasks of mourning." Let's take an even closer look at these as we consider not only the major losses from loved ones' deaths, but also all other significant losses.

After totally acknowledging and accepting the change or loss, we need to be present, aware, and really experience the pain of this loss. Having accepted or at least acknowledged the loss, our next task is to experience the pain associated with the loss—whether in sadness, physical and mental suffering, forced solitude, or difficult thoughts and feelings. These can include feelings of anger or fear, a sense of abandonment, a void within our daily routines. We may become aware of a feeling of numbness, a loss of focus, an increase in physical fatigue. We may experience shortness of breath, a sense of emptiness, etc. After accepting and experiencing the pain, we are then open to the task and opportunity of slowly adjusting to the loss. We can slowly adapt to life as it has become, without the who—or the what—that we have lost.

We may not like it, but we need to adapt. This adaptation is absolutely necessary to work through our grief at this stage. Adapting means adjusting; it also means accommodating. It does not mean returning to what was. What it does mean is accommodation to a new life. We have to live in the "new normal," as the catchphrase has it.

Finally, we hopefully reach the place where we can slowly reinvest in this new life, this "new normal." We learn to reengage with life, to connect, reconnect, and recommit with both old and new relationships. We find that we can catch our breath, reaching a new base camp and a place of hope. We come to a place where we can now move forward from the losses, the negative events, and the changes we have endured. We don't simply move on, but we move ahead—through the grief, the major disruptions, and the disappointments in life—growing as we do. We grieve, yes, but we grow. And that growth may take us ahead in amazing and totally new directions.

I have spent a lot of time writing here on the tasks of working through grief for growth and transformation. While grieving the death of a loved one is undoubtedly the largest manner of loss that we experience—with varying degrees of difficulty due to the particular or unique circumstances of any loss—there are well over forty types of losses that can introduce grief: remember, "change = loss = grief." I vividly remember that after my parents died, I deeply grieved their deaths. I grieved their aging in their 80s which was accompanied by their increasing infirmity and the loss of their independence. Then it fell upon me, their last remaining descendant, to manage the disbandment of their home and possessions, which forced me to deal with the tasks of mourning once again, against the backdrop of their belongings, collections, and "stuff." Forced to decide what to keep, what to sell, what to share, and what to throw away, I experienced additional pain, trying to adjust to something which I had never experienced before. I needed to take the time to process what I could for my personal growth in this new life without them. So, here was acceptance, pain, and attempts to adapt. But what about reinvesting and reconnecting with others?

Here is where it all came apart. (Only later was I able to knit things together in a new way.) After my parents died, I was confronted with—and needed to accept—this fact: that in my early 50s, divorced, single, having had no children, with both of my siblings and now both of my parents gone, I had no immediate family. I felt that I had no one above me, no one beside me, and no one below or following me. I felt truly alone, abandoned, and literally orphaned. Someone had once said that you don't fully become an adult until your second parent has died. I can still recall that moment when I reached that point. I had the image of being held face down in the mud by God, seemingly hearing the words, "Have you had enough yet?" But even then, at that moment, it felt more benevolent than malevolent. From that came my humility; I recalled that the words "humbled" and "humility" come from the same root word for dirt or earth. This was a moment of transformation for me. I admitted then and there that I had had enough, and gave in, or opened up, to my faith and to divine power and direction. Quite suddenly, or so it seemed, the pain was just gone. I lost my sense of victimhood and stopped envying others for their relationships and possessions. I was in that time and space in between the endings and beginnings, what William Bridges termed as "the neutral zone."[4] Somehow, I felt strangely supported, despite not having a family. I felt numb, yet comforted.

Then, within a few weeks after that I experienced another "peak experience,"[5] a moment of transcendence that moved me above and beyond who I was. I was at an airport terminal, heading for a connecting flight, when, surrounded by hundreds or thousands of other travelers—all strangers to me—I stopped and stepped back from the pedestrian traffic. As I looked around, I was suddenly able to look at the crowd, the flow of travelers, seeing them all as fellow pilgrims, as brothers and sisters, parents and children, as loved ones with whom I felt kinship. I realized in that moment that I loved them all, and the loneliness and sense of separation evaporated. I was connected—and re-connected again—to others. In a way, I experienced a personal "kintsugi." My brokenness was "reknit"—and it was made more beautiful through the preciousness and the transformation of the repairs.

> *"The emotional reaction in the peak experience has a special flavor of wonder, of awe, of reverence, of humility and surrender before the experience as before something great."* —Abraham Maslow

I have since been told of others' experiences of transformation and transcendence following not only their loved ones' deaths, but other significant losses, including various negative life events. One man shared with me how his mother's passing "into calm eternity" was the most spiritual experience that he had ever had. Another described the dawn of the day after his career position was eliminated as something "transcendent," with a new lightness of being and a deepened sense of gratitude. About six months after my dad had died, I remember standing in the shower and feeling what seemed to be a hand on my shoulder, with the assurance that "I'm okay." I strongly sensed this as a message of assurance from my dad, who had struggled with his faith ever since his firstborn, my big sister, Ann had died. That moment of assurance gave me a sense that he really was okay, and it very much was a defining moment of comfort and transcendence for me.

Having to say goodbye—whether to a loved one through their death, a special relationship, a job that you loved or needed, a home that you grew up in, a marriage in which you had great hope and plans for the future, or any number of things that represent a significant loss or change in a familiar pattern of being—is a hard thing. There is certainly no doubting that. When they choose to grace us, these transcendent glimpses of assurance are truly welcome.

Letting go of possessions—one's own, or those of loved ones—can also take us down the path of loss and grief, yet it can also be a place where we can experience transformation—and even transcendence. We can—through these changes and losses, through these things taken away and let go of—grow even above and beyond where we are in faith, toward a greater understanding, and into a deeper sense of connection with all beings and the earth. While it may be difficult to imagine—in light of our modern, industrialized order's push towards the "gaining and the getting" of consumerism, and in light of peer pressure and "influencers"—that we can actually grow through the paradox of letting go, of gaining through giving. Some years ago, I heard the invitation to donate to a fundraiser with the words, "Give until it hurts." I later realized the opposite was true: we "give until it feels good." The first statement suggests pain as a motivator; the second, joy. As children we develop paradigms, mental schemas or structures, that guide us in learning how to choose and act. As adolescents and young adults, we slowly become more comfortable with wrestling with paradox, the seemingly illogical situation of two contrasting things or concepts that are both true. But there's more. When I was discussing the matter with a close friend, together we realized that between "paradigm" and "paradox" we can find "paradise"—at least in the Merriam-Webster Dictionary!

> *"If you are seeking a time when you will be finished, you will never be done."* —Tibetan saying

So yes, gather, of course. Grieve when you must. Let go. Let it be. Give until it feels good. Help others. Continue on the path of healing, and permit the paradox of growth through release. Grow with a lighter load, but with an illumined or fuller heart, with the light that shines even in the darkness. Move towards your core values and commit to action for the sake of the people, purpose, mission, faith, and spirituality of your life. While doing so, allow yourself to experience joy and contentment over simple pleasures. Integrate new passions and companions with select and especially meaningful possessions that you truly value and treasure. Grow by discovering new attitudes, with a heightened sensitivity toward others and their feelings. Grow through gaining new insights, with the firm understanding that things are replaceable, but people aren't.

CHAPTER 13
THE SEVENTEENTH DAY; CLOSING THE JOURNAL
AND HEADING HOME

> *"Let's look at what we've written
> and decide that these are not pipe dreams;
> these are our marching orders.
> These are the blueprints for our lives."*
> —Glennon Doyle

Prior to a well-deserved sleep, Rob had pulled up his Order of St. Romanus personal "rule of life" on his laptop, and then added the new values and disciplines derived from his time at St. Cecilia's. He had wanted to visit with Sr. Margaret once more but learned that she had left for a seminar at Creighton University in Omaha, a three-hour drive north of the monastery, and wasn't expected back until evening. After his morning routine, Rob began the task of packing to return home. He left his "cell" as spotless as he had found it, except for three things which he placed on the desk. One was a note for Sr. Margaret, thanking her for her unselfish ministry, her patience, her holding space for him in their sessions, and for her prayers. Their sessions together had allowed him the opportunity to go deeper into heartfelt stirrings that provided him both a foundation and an unlimited "head and heart space." On the desk he also left his check for the lodging and his love offering for Sr. Margaret's gift of spiritual direction. Finally, he placed a symbolic "leave behind" gift of his time in the house. Pilgrims traveling the Camino de Santiago in Spain[1] leave small stones at the Iron Cross, symbolically letting go of something that needs to be released. Rob also wanted to leave something behind, and he had no difficulty in deciding what to leave. He reached inside his shoulder bag and located a small Ziplock bag with his large gold James Avery cross ring that had been a parting gift from his former wife Meg all those many years ago. He opened the bag, and instead of selling the ring as he had planned, placed it inside the envelope with his check and laid it on the desk next to the note and the door key. Then, as an afterthought, he grabbed a small scrap of paper and quickly scribbled out an "IOU" for the sisters, promising them copies of his book after it was published.

With that, he gathered his things, stripped the bed, stuffed the linens in the pillowcase, and set them outside the door in the hallway as was customary. After collecting the small bag of trash, he laid the key on the desk, grabbed his bags, laptop, and manuscript, and walked out into the sunshine. After taking the trash and the recyclables from his room to the bins behind the guesthouse, he went to his car and found the reminders of his earlier wakeup call in the back seat and the trunk: the junk. Rob slowly—and mindfully—gathered it all, separated it according to where it now needed to go, with his work files and the small bag of papers needing to be shred placed behind the front seats, the box of books to donate slid to the left side of the trunk, and the car items moved to the right side of the trunk.

After removing the bags of trash and recyclables, he carried them over to their respective bins, blissfully tossing them in with an incredible sense of relief and satisfaction. Looking into the spaciousness of the trunk, Rob suddenly felt as if he had grown a foot taller and sensed a clearer mind and a lighter heart. This was reward enough, he thought, as he now knew, without regret or a shadow of doubt, that his resolve to go through life from here on with a clean trunk—the metaphor for his life—was confirmed. And while not a full-time resident member of a religious community, he could now go home and apply the reflections, lessons, and strategies that he had learned here to his life outside the monastery's walls.

A changed man, transformed, he got into the car, started the engine, and clicked his seat belt in place. Putting the car in gear, he began the drive home in silence, with an inner peace he had not felt for many years, perhaps recalling some aspects of those early years in the Army and college. He reflected back for a moment, and then also looked ahead, with a transcendent and deeply felt peace of acceptance, gratitude, and freedom.

EPILOGUE

> *"Short of taking monastic vows*
> *or trekking into the Kalahari,*
> *a freighter passage might just offer*
> *what our relentlessly connected age*
> *has made difficult, if not impossible:*
> *splendid isolation."*
> —Christopher Buckley

In the twelve months since his retreat, Rob had learned that the decision had been made by the prioress of St. Cecilia's to tear down the aging and slowly crumbling Administration Hall, due to its condition and the high cost of maintaining and repairing it. Reportedly, the demolition had already begun in recent weeks, after the sisters had removed everything that was valuable and usable elsewhere on the campus. Learning of this through the community's recently emailed newsletter, Rob was somewhat prepared for what he thought he might find after deciding that he would return for a half-day visit and a session with Sr. Margaret.

Has it really been a year already? Rob wondered. As he drove the two hours from his home to St. Cecilia's, he began to review how different his life had become in the months since his self-sequestering and writing. Having added to his personal rule, he had sought to continue to live out the rule as an "extended community married monastic lay associate," which is how he self-identified. In addition, he was also now an author. His book based on his journal was in the final edits and was expected to be published soon. Leaving his fulltime position—this time by choice—he returned to offering occasional pastoral service, part-time teaching, and continuing to build upon and deepen from his time of spiritual formation at "the Mount."

After returning home from the monastery the previous year, Rob had implemented some additional meaningful spiritual practices. He began each day by greeting the dawn with gratitude to God as Infinite, Intimate, and In-dwelling[1], a more personal Trinitarian view that seemed to resonate with him. Brief morning prayer followed before arising, and then attending to personal care prior to starting a pot of coffee. Rob used this morning time as a golden hour for contemplative prayer, followed by a review of his rule, his daily rewriting of his top goals, and a look at his calendar for the day.

After a simple breakfast of juice, coffee, and toast with Rachel, Rob would read out loud the morning service and scripture verses from the Book of Common Prayer. Typically, the shared to-do list and their day's schedules of appointments would follow. After Rachel left for work, Rob would typically retreat to his study for writing, and, of course, more reading. While the room's appearance and ambience were far from that of a centuries' old monastery, it did serve as a suitable container for his "inner monastery." Like the "Holodeck" on the *Star Trek:*

Next Generation TV series,[2] he could imagine and interact with this virtual monastery in any way that he wanted. Rob had visualized his special place of retreat with heavy oak doors, a panoramic view of a forest, and the lulling sounds of a babbling brook. Yet, in his study and surrounded by his favorite and frequently referenced books, accessible and displayed in the tall wood bookcases, he found he rarely had to imagine anyplace else. In his study sat his comfortable reading chairs, along with an undated second-hand dark wood desk and the large oak wardrobe from the late 1800s that often called to mind for visitors the wardrobe from the C.S. Lewis *Narnia* story.[3] The south and west-facing windows with views of the home's wooded lot helped tremendously as Rob continued to gain a "Be ... here ... now" outlook, which he considered a special gift from his time at St. Cecilia's and his expansion of his rule.

Sometimes he took a walk through the large, old oak tree-filled neighborhood, and sometimes not. Visits to local coffee shops as "mini-retreats"—often to reflect and write—became frequent. Years before, even when single and living in a clean, minimalist one-bedroom apartment, Rob would often walk to a nearby coffee shop and find a booth for journaling. Phone calls and online meetings for spiritual companioning and grief support were scheduled and typically conducted in the study, which had served as a virtual office for all his sessions and meetings. And although "sensory rich," the study still conveyed to his online clients an uncluttered and comforting view for grief work, spiritual companionship, and the visioning and planning work for their spiritual and psychological "right-sizing" and "pre-death cleaning."

Of course, as books, magazines, and correspondence arrived by mail or a delivery service, Rob sought to follow the "One in, one out" guideline (and at times, "one in, two out"). Selective and purposeful shedding and thinning of old possessions, paperwork, things to share, donate, sell, or recycle continued. Over the past year he and Rachel had assigned themselves one major area of the purposeful thinning work for each month, deciding on one month for closets, one month for the garage, and another for the attic, and so forth. Paper and photos from the basement were brought up and thinned while watching TV or listening to music. An additional blue recycling container for the curbside was found, and other papers were taken to shredding events when they were held at the church. Little by little, they were finding more space available for greater peace of mind and came to enjoy their discoveries in the old files and family photos. And each week, after taking a small bag of trash out for trash pickup, the little that was left from the kitchen was put into the new compost bin in the yard, near the rain barrels for the home's lawn and garden watering.

In addition, as both he and Rachel became more selective in their social network, efforts continued to connect with the smaller subsets of close friends and a small—but growing—secondary circle of like-minded others. Rachel and Rob also continued to grow in their mutual healing paths of reviewing, resolving, rediscovering, reducing, reinvesting, and renewing. Rob was living by his rule in a more mindful and purposeful way than at any time prior, and Rachel began a discernment process for her own personal rule of life.

Other than the life-changing drive to St. Cecilia's the prior year (that included the tire blowout and the wakeup call of his trunk), Rob had always enjoyed the solitary drive to the Mount, and the drive was almost always undertaken in silence. In returning this time, when he reached the point where State Road 47 shifted to due north, with farmland and some small lakes to the west and the railroad lines to the east, Rob came into view of the spot where, one year before, his tire had blown out, leading to his wakeup call to identify and let go of what was no longer needed in his life. He smiled to himself, shaking his head almost in disbelief, recalling that wakeup call of the collection of stuff in his trunk, and the vivid memory of his stack of papers being swept up and tossed by the wind into the pond. Thinking back, it was like he had been a different person then; truth be told, perhaps he was.

As he approached the monastery, driving up the narrow driveway that slowly curved and led up the hill toward Mount St. Cecilia's, he quickly noticed a glaring gap between some of the buildings on the campus. There, between the convent and the Sophia Center and library, was an empty space where the Administration Hall used to stand. Pulling into the parking lot, he saw the pile of remains of what was left of the building, old structural beams, brick and stone, along with concrete, pieces of flooring, plaster walls, and even a broken ceiling fan from one of the community rooms where Rob had often gathered with others for study and prayer. As this was Sunday afternoon, and with no one from the demolition crew present on site, Rob squeezed through a gap in the chain link fence and looked around, trying his best to take it all in.

It really seemed all too much to try to absorb. He recalled how the convent had done some remodeling years before and had offered the fold-up wooden auditorium seats for sale. Rob had quickly picked out a row of three connecting seats, gave the office manager his check for the suggested (and extremely reasonable) love offering of $30, disassembled them, and somehow managed to fit them inside his car. He was especially glad that he had saved those seats, seeing the building now demolished. A pile of rubble was all that remained of what was once a large and impressive building which had served as a spiritual gathering place for study and community. An indelible memory began to come to the surface from back when he had started the program at St. Cecilia's. On his first day there, as he walked up to the building for that very first time, he was overwhelmed at seeing and entering the imposing century-old building. Now, he recalled—perhaps in a prescient way—that after a few months in the program, as he walked up to the same building after breakfast, the building had seemed to almost disappear in his imagination, with the students and sisters present, but no building surrounding them or holding them up. Now, it was like that had come true. The building was gone, but he knew that the people and the programs remained. The Sophia Center and library had been repurposed to house the program of spiritual companioning, containing many of the artifacts, artwork, and furniture items from the old building. The summer internships and weekend programs continued and were now all based in the former library. Rob came to very much realize that buildings were built to serve people, and not for their own sake. He saw that the only constant was change. He also saw in the community's decision and action the sisters' acceptance and their adapting to this change and loss. While the Administration Hall would be no more, the community's work would continue. Walking through the rubble, he looked down and happened to spot a few chunks of what he quickly recognized as the building's terrazzo marble flooring. This was the flooring that he had remembered so often walking on. So many times in prayer, as he lowered his gaze to his feet, had he focused on the flooring's interesting and colorful patterns! Reaching down, he selected a few pieces, rubbed the concrete dust from the small surviving sections, and put them in his pocket. These would become his artifacts from St. Cecilia's.

As he turned and walked away, remembering his spiritual direction appointment with Sr. Margaret, he resolved to not only continue to practice what he had learned, but to share what he learned with others: While possessions—and structures—are important, the focus firmly needs to be on the *priority of people* and the *proper use of possessions and structures*—never the other way around. The sun's rays bathed Rob in warmth as he walked toward the Sophia Center, his new place of "fresh springs," for his meeting with the sister. And as he had done with Rachel on a regular basis, he now looked forward to sharing with Sr. Margaret all that he had learned about belonging, connection, purpose, grief, possessions, and the growth that is possible through all of these. As well, he looked forward to telling the sister of his call to dedicate his life to guide and companion others in their own opportunities for transformation and transcendence.

JOURNALING GUIDE FOR PART IV: LIGHTENING UP
CHAPTERS 12–13

1. Considering growth from brokenness—when have I been hurt, broken, abandoned, bereaved, and am now able to look back and see my growth?
2. From which events or losses have I become stronger in the broken places? Name one or two and write a paragraph on each.
3. Are there any peak experiences that I have had which have come out of a loss or a disruption of my life? What were they?
4. Name any experiences where I have felt lighter as a result of letting go of things that I was struggling with, or that were holding me back. A bad job? Outdated or ill-fitting clothes? Junk or clutter? Old dreams or desires?
5. Have there been times where I gave until it felt good? List a few ways in which I could do that today or this week.
6. What might be one thing I could do today or this week to experience and document my personal

transformative growth in reclaiming my life's space from unwanted and unneeded things?
7. What might be a repurposing gift, or any other kind of purposeful relinquishment of items, that I could make?

JOURNALING GUIDE FOR THE EPILOGUE

Finding a place to be quiet, alone, and relaxed, either in a physical or imagined visualized "happy place," journal about what life is like one year from now. Here are some suggestions:

Imagine this future date now, and journal how far you have come, how your life has changed, how you have not only weathered the storm, but have "grown stronger in the broken places."

List your places of growth in your living a lighter yet more meaningful life—in having not just your basic needs satisfied, but also the higher-level needs of purpose, belonging, connection and meaning.

How much richer is life for you now, and with those around you? What new ways have you found to give? How have you lightened your load?

In which ways have you progressed on the realization of worthy goals and ideals?

What are some ways that you have experienced happiness? How have you experienced—or at least had glimpses of—joy and transcendent or peak experiences of moving above and beyond yourself?

What positive and healthy routines have you begun or continued — physically, socially, spiritually, mentally?

What about the space around you? Is it cleaner, less cluttered? Closets and drawers —are they more organized or spacious now?

Are there fewer attention units spent on nagging distractions, and more attention units available for the important things and people in your life?

Summing up your journal and work in this epilogue: Where is your new growth and "be-ing" now, with some evidence of your old life gone and living your new life now?

Suggestion: Journal as you visualize this future, taking as many paragraphs or pages as you need. As often as you journal, include—or at least be open to—what you have visualized here as you work toward your own progressive realization of your worthy goals and ideals. On a regular basis—whether monthly, weekly, daily, or sporadically—let this visualization direct and guide your goal setting and your positive habits as you work toward a lighter and a less cluttered future.

APPENDICES

ROB'S RULE

When Rob was accepted as a Lay Associate of the Order of St. Romanus,[1] he had been tasked with the discernment and work of developing a personal rule of life, based on the Benedictine rule to which all affiliated orders and associates pledge to live by. Lay associates, of course, were afforded more latitude, as they weren't living in the monastic community as celibate members of the order. Still, it was something that Rob took seriously, and prior to his installation as an associate, he developed his own rule to guide his life. A "rule" was considered not so much like a law, but rather as a guide or a railing to help guide and support an individual and a community. A rule can also be conceived of as a template, a touchstone, a map, or an agenda for life. It can be dedicated and serve as a commitment to not only oneself and others in one's community, but to God and all other living beings. From the rule the desires and intentions for spiritual practices and growth can flow, aligned with the core values, and lived out through the disciplines with stewardship for others, self, and the world. Over his discernment year, Rob crafted his rule, building upon the order's three principles of Obedience, Stability, and Conversion of Life. After adding a fourth principle of Gratitude, Rob defined and elaborated on his core values as those being most relevant and meaningful. Finally, the last section of his rule listed and provided short descriptions of his disciplines, or how he learned and practiced the principles and the values.

Rob's rule always accompanied him to retreats and those infrequent vacations, and this retreat—although a working one—had been no exception. While much of his rule was long internalized, his review of it during the unfolding of his time in the guest house and his journaling revealed some things that were not part of his existing rule. As a result of his wake-up call, and the writing that flowed from pen to paper, and then on to his laptop in his guest room, Rob came to realize that his rule needed an addendum. As he had only recently updated his original rule for the order's Director of Associates—as was requested of all associates for their renewal of their vows in their annual report—Rob decided he would build upon his original rule with new insights and values. These new insights and values now integrated with his learnings, validations, and the disciplines he realized he needed in his moving forward. As an adjunct to his journal and this guidebook, here are both his original rule and the addendum:

ROBERT MICHAEL SHAW'S "RULE OF LIFE"

MY PRINCIPLES

Obedience—*Asking, listening, and responding to God's call in my life.*

Stability—*In prayer, service to others, work/life balance, personal time, and in marriage.*

Conversion of life—*Through 1) prayer and study for closeness with God, 2) maturing in marriage and 3) in further professional and vocational development.*

Gratitude—*Thankfulness and gratitude for God's love, grace, and blessings.*

MY VALUES

Connection with God—*Accepting and living in God's love and grace, in hope and faith, and in enjoying God's pleasures.*

Connection with others—*Developing and maintaining positive connections with family, friends, colleagues, and my neighbors. Greater awareness and action, with kindness and healthy boundaries, within and through my True Self versus my false self.*

Hospitality—*In openness, warmth, and in more social and remote events with others.*

Humility—*Being more honest, self-accepting, and transparent with self and others.*

Education—*Seeking out education and learning, and then applying these new learnings. Learning and growing both as a student and as an educator.*

Balance—*A work/life balance, fostering recognition and empowerment of head and heart.*

Mindfulness—*Being more aware, and in seeing God in all things and in others.*

Health—*Fitness, with purposeful quality movement, diet, and sleep. Freedom from illness/disease. Good mental health, full senses, and joy.*

Financial Integrity—*Debt free, with savings/investments of God's resources and income, being able to share resources with the church, schools, and charitable organizations.*

Peace of Mind—*From fear or worry; able to let things go and to receive their blessings.*

MY DISCIPLINES

Personal Prayer—*Morning contemplative prayer and Compline. Re-grounding through quiet time and mindfulness.*

Self-Examination—*Journaling, dream work, counseling, and spiritual direction. With possessions, thoughtfully reviewing what I need to keep and what I should release.*

Study—*Continue studies and work in spirituality and coaching. Reading one book each week. Study and work in spiritual and grief coaching, Welcoming Prayer, and spiritual direction.*

Connection with others—*Loving Rachel and the children and grandchildren, offering them the space to be who they are and desire to be. Staying connected with my cousins. Developing and maintaining positive connections with friends and with those whom I serve. Interacting more with greater kindness and healthy boundaries.*

Mindfulness—*Being more aware, attentive, and non-judging. Seeing God in all things and in others. Living more in the present moment, with my past of losses and gains left in the past.*

Health—*Purposeful movement, diet, and sleep. Freedom from illness/disease. Good mental health, full senses, and joy. Following physicians' orders and best practices. 12-14 plant-based food servings and whole grains weekly. Plenty of clean water for adequate hydration. 3-5 walks each week, with a 3-mile walk during the weekend.*

Financial Integrity—*Continuing the practice of being debt free, with savings and investments of God's resources, and the sharing of resources with others.*

Stewardship—*Continue in conservative work as a good steward of various resources, and in continuing to work through my parents' and my own old files, photos, and keepsakes.*

Rejuvenation—*Coffee (with self and others), retreats, regular date nights, and long weekends and vacations. Finding and using a "cabin" for retreat (real or virtual).*

Pilgrimage[1]—*Train, fundraise, and take the bicycling trip in the next year, donating the money to the March of Dimes in memory of Ann.*

Mission—*To care for others (without forgetting self), and to succeed as self (without hurting others). Continue work with a healthy balance. To maximize my potential from God in ways that bring honor and glory to God. To feel God's pleasure in how I live my life.*

ROB'S RULE ADDENDUM: SIMPLICITY & STEWARDSHIP

CORE VALUES

Absolute awareness — awakening to awareness and using it for good.

Openness to God and others — to God's direction; to the bids and asks of others.

Acceptance of abundance — of what I have in my possession, both tangible and intangible.

Generosity — to others as to self.

Love for the earth — working and living in alignment with this earth, our fragile island home.

Healthy authority & personal agency — in serving as "scaffolding," or a "lattice of love" for others.

Quality — in both the physical and the metaphysical sense.

Simplicity — *the order and appreciation of how "less" can be "more."*

Growing through grief — *in the ways that working through loss and grief can be transformative for self and in helping others.*

Openness to mystery — *open to experiencing greater illumination and transcendence in the liminal space of mystery.*

DISCIPLINES

- *Acknowledging, accepting, and adapting as needed.*
- *Bi-weekly online spiritual education and fellowship groups.*
- *Confessing, repenting, reconciling, and restoring.*
- *Daily contemplative meditation.*
- *Daily reading, reading one book per week; daily writing, averaging 800 words per day.*
- *Experiencing, feeling, and living authentically.*
- *Giving of my time, within limits, in spiritual coaching and teaching.*
- *Listening daily to the Jesuits' "Pray as You Go" app.*
- *Mindful divestment of things not needed: "Keep, share, sell; determine what to donate, recycle, and trash."*
- *Narrowing the social field and enlarging the smaller subset of friends.*
- *Thinning, using the purposeful shedding process, regularly sorting, and releasing "things" that I have held onto and accumulated, with more of these things going out than coming in.*
- *Walking the healing path of enlightened stewardship: resolve, review, reduce, reinvest, renew.*

- *Weekly church attendance and reaching out to those in my secondary circle of friends and associates for friendship, collaboration, and for community.*

CREATING YOUR OWN RULE OF LIFE

Here is an adapted and simplified style from the Rule of Benedict for creating your own rule:

1. Principles. Principles can be your highest propositions, truths, aspirations, rules, or prime directives, which form your foundations for life. Examples might be *obedience* to God or your True Self; *stability* in life, career, or marriage/committed relationships; *conversion* of life, as in changing from self-neglect or abuse to self-care, or a deepening in faith and spiritual practice; and *gratitude*, in thankfulness, blessing God and others in return.

2. Values. Values would be your core values for life — what it is that exemplifies your life, with examples such as connection with God, connection with others, purpose and meaning, hospitality, good health, lifelong learning, and preservation of family records and heirlooms.

3. Disciplines. These are those things that you consistently do in living through your adhering to your principles and core values; they support and help make real your principles and values. Examples might be simplicity, keeping a clean home and work space, developing and maintaining healthy relationships, good self-care, belonging to a faith community, caring for others, being debt-free, meditating or daily prayer, reading, journaling, daily movement or exercise, honoring or paying tribute to others, or purposeful shedding of what you don't need.

In a nutshell, *your rule is putting in writing—and dedicating yourself to—what you believe is most sacred, valued, desired, and practiced.*

And, once done, regularly read your rule, updating it yearly and whenever needed.

NOTES

1. THE DRIVE

1. While the term "convent" has traditionally been used to designate a cloistered women's community and buildings, many are now using the term "monastery" for both men's and women's communities. There also are some communities such as John Michael Talbot's "Brothers and Sisters of Charity" in Arkansas which includes celibate brothers, celibate sisters, singles (who can marry), as well as families. At their Little Portion Hermitage, there are common work areas yet separate cloistered areas for each of the groupings.
2. "All my springs of joy are in you." Psalm 87:7, Christian Standard Bible.
3. Compline prayer is the Anglican/Episcopal Church's night prayer found in the Book of Common Prayer, to be used at the completion of the day.
4. Episcopal Church (1979). *The Book of Common Prayer* and administration of the sacraments and other rites and ceremonies of the church: together with the Psalter or Psalms of David according to the use of the Episcopal Church. New York: Seabury Press. *The Book of Common Prayer*, dating back to 1549 in England, continues with occasional updates to serve as the communal book of worship services and prayers across the Anglican/Episcopal communion in over 50 countries.

2. THE DAY OF SELF-AWARENESS AND LOOKING BACK

1. "In twenty years or so ..." Apparently, our calendar re-sequences every 28 years, except for some exceptions due to leap years.
2. *The Book of Common Prayer* (see 1-4 above).
3. "Order of St. Romanus." This monastic order is fictional.

3. THE NEXT MORNING; THE JOURNAL BEGINS

1. "1-800-Go Trash." Not a real company; suggests trash service companies in general.

4. THE "WHYS" AND THE "WHATS" OF COLLECTING AND KEEPING

1. The classic 1941 American film *Citizen Kane*, a quasi-biographical story of William Randolph Hearst and his crowd, dramatized the accumulation of possessions, even some from childhood.
2. The Diagnostic and Statistical Manual of Mental Disorders, 5th edition.
3. Rachel Kodanaz, Finding peace, one piece at a time: What to do with your and a loved one's personal possessions (Fulcrum Publishing 2019).
4. Allison Gilbert, Passed and present: Keeping memories of loved ones alive (Seal Press (2016).

5. THE REWARDS OF OBTAINING, COLLECTING, ACCUMULATING, AND HOLDING ON TO THINGS

1. Abraham Maslow, "A theory of human motivation," *The Psychological Review*, (1943).

6. CHANGE = LOSS = GRIEF

1. Grief Recovery Method is an evidence-based grief recovery program developed and conducted by the Grief Recovery Institute. Their website is www.griefrecoverymethod.com.

7. THE WORK

1. One of the possible interpretations of the camel and "the eye of a needle" suggested the small openings at the gates of ancient cities. The mention is found in the Christian scriptures' New Testament gospels of Matthew 19:24.
2. The Pareto Principle, referred to as the 80/20 rule, suggests that roughly 80% of outcomes are derived from 20% of the work. It has also been used conversely, suggesting situations where 20% of the work takes 80% of the time.
3. Margareta Magnusson, The gentle art of Swedish death cleaning: How to free yourself and your family from a lifetime of clutter (Scribner, (2018).
4. Kodanaz, op. cit
5. Judi Culbertson and Marj Decker, *Scaling down: Living large in a smaller space.* (Rodale, 2005).

6. Gilbert, op, cit.
7. Magnusson, op. cit.

8. GETTING HELP

1. T. McKechnie, *The last chapter: Documenting your pre-and post-death decisions.* Counseling Connections, 2019. The website for *The Last Chapter* book can be found at https://www.lastchapterbook.com
2. A. Schneiderman, Adam Seifer, and G. Newman, *In case you get hit by a bus: How to organize your life now for when you're not around later.* (Workman Publishing, 2020).
3. Check in your area to see what services are available for eco-friendly recycling and disposal of unwanted items and trash.

9. SELF CARE OF BODY, MIND, AND SOUL

1. Maslow, op. cit.
2. *Clutter's Last Stand* is Don Aslett's blunt, honest, "no holds barred" approach book series written to help readers deal with clutter.
3. David Steindl-Rast, The music of silence. (HarperSanFrancisco, 1995).
4. The character Mr. Spock's greeting for wishing another well on the original *Star Trek TV* series. The phrase had apparently been adapted by Leonard Nimoy from Jewish and Arabic greetings.
5. Cynthia Bourgeault, *Centering prayer and inner awakening.* (Cowley Publications, 2004).
6. Jon Kabat-Zinn, Wherever you go there you are: Mindfulness meditation in everyday life. (Hyperion, 1994).
7. E. Tolle, The power of now: A guide to spiritual enlightenment (Yellow Kite, (2016).

10. THE PATH OF HEALING AND GROWTH

1. The concept of "attention units" was featured in Jack Canfield's *Self Esteem and Peak Performance* seminar audio programs from CareerTrack (1990). Canfield gave the term to those thoughts that nag us or remind us of things like clutter, disorganization, and unfinished projects, diverting away our attention and energy. These may cause us to move into the double-negative state of "I need to or have to ... clean out that closet, etc. ... but I can't right now ...").
2. J. W. Worden, Grief counseling and grief therapy: A handbook for the mental health professional (5th ed.) (Springer Publishing Company, 2018).

11. SIMPLICITY

1. The Ed Sullivan Show was a variety TV show on CBS from 1948 to 1971. His acts ranged from specialty performers like Eric Brenn and his plates to groups such as The Beatles.
2. The 1993 American film Groundhog Day portrayed the main character as a mean-spirited, depressed, and self-centered TV weatherman who keeps reliving the same day until he gets it right.
3. Charles Barsotti was a famous cartoonist who drew nearly 1400 cartoons for *The New Yorker* magazine from the 1960s to 2014. His cartoons often featured a small, cute dog.
4. Psalm 46:10; Revised Standard Version of the Bible.
5. *Let it Be* by Paul McCartney and The Beatles, was written during and released after The Beatles break up in 1970. In 1969 *Let it Be* also was the name of The Beatles' final album as a group.

12. GROWTH THROUGH LETTING GO

1. Compline prayer (see 1-3 above).
2. E. Hemingway, *A farewell to arms* (Vintage Classics, 1999).
3. Genesis 32:22-32. Revised Standard Version Bible.
4. W. Bridges, Transitions: making sense of life's changes. (Addison-Wesley, 1980).
5. "Peak experiences" were named and discussed by both William James (The varieties of religious experience: A study in human nature) and later Abraham Maslow ("Cognition of Being in the Peak Experiences," J. Genetic Psychol., 1959, 94, 43–66. Also A. H. Maslow, Motivation and Personality, op. cit.

13. THE SEVENTEENTH DAY; CLOSING THE JOURNAL

1. The "Cruz de Ferro" is an iron cross atop a tall wooden pole at the highest point of a French part of the historic and celebrated pilgrimage route, Camino de Santiago, in Spain. Pilgrims typically leave a small stone at the cross to symbolize something or someone that they are letting go of or releasing.

EPILOGUE

1. Paul Smith, Integral Christianity: The Spirit's Call to Evolve (Paragon Press, 2011).
2. The fictional "holodeck", described as a holographic environmental simulator, was conceived and used in the *Star Trek: Next generation* TV series, which aired from 1987 to 1994.
3. C. S. Lewis, The lion, the witch, and the wardrobe. (Geoffrey Bles, 1950).

ROB'S RULE

1. A fictional monastic order.

ROBERT MICHAEL SHAW'S "RULE OF LIFE"

1. A pilgrimage typically involves making a trip, usually one of some effort and length, with special significance or devotion. For some it is travel to a holy site such as Lourdes or Mecca, and for others it might be Graceland. Some make special trips as commemorative or memorial trips in memory of a loved one, a beloved place, or as part of a life review.

ACKNOWLEDGMENTS

This book invariably grew from my family of origin's story, along with the blessings and the sorrows, both the universal and the unique. There were also, of course, the things and items that we possessed, were given, and those special ones that were intentionally collected and treasured. I have learned much from both the *people* and the *possessions* about belonging, connection, and meaning.

As I was growing up, my parents owned a small print shop in St. Louis, which they referred to as their "publishing company." After some years they got into paperback books; not just for reading, but for selling. They became distributors to schools and retail outlets, and then opened and ran a few small bookstores as independent booksellers. I grew up surrounded by books, and was entertained, enriched, and educated by the stories and wisdom they held within. So it was probably not a surprise that my first sales position after completing my tour of duty as an Army medic was with a medical publishing company.

Years later, in my work as a hospice grief specialist (or "bereavement coordinator," as if through the calls, mailings, groups, and visits I could somehow "coordinate" the deceased patients' loved ones' grief), I was encouraged by my colleagues Vickie Mears, Jeff O'Dell, and Therese McKechnie to make a presentation to the Grief Support Network group in Kansas

City on the connection that I saw between grief and possessions. As well, Dr. Harold Ivan Smith, a talented researcher and author whom I am proud to call friend, was the first to say to me, "I *really* think that there is a book in this!" The spark was lit and then fanned into a flame by these encouraging colleagues.

I need to also acknowledge and thank Mr. John Jackson, my journalism teacher and school newspaper advisor from Roosevelt High. It was through Mr. Jackson that, in my being named the Editor-in-Chief my senior year, I learned some foundational rules for reporting, writing, editing, creating artwork, cutting & pasting, team collaboration, publication, marketing, and distribution. The skillful advisement that I received proved to be an outstanding foundation for my entry into my collegiate pre-journalism program the following fall.

My early experiences in journalism were rekindled later by my friend and colleague Jonathan Hyde, a journalism major (and later a journalism teacher for an urban high school, which was not unlike my own Roosevelt High), who along with his wife, Peggy Sullivan, a child psychologist, provided much-needed encouragement, support, and valuable guidance in my writing.

From all my places of higher learning, there are many to thank, yet too numerous to name. You all have been skillful guides for me.

I also want to acknowledge those authors, songwriters, poets, and people of great character and insight from whom I have learned and have been inspired by their lives and their words over the years: Og Mandino, Joni Mitchell, Rev. Matthew Fox, Paul Simon, Rumi, Khalil Gibran, Rev. Margaret Guenther, James Taylor, Jimmy Carter, Natalie Merchant, M. Scott Peck, John Sebastian, Alan Alda, Anne Lamott, Mark Knopfler, David

Byrne, Temple Grandin, Robert Pirsig, and Rev. Richard Rohr, OFM.

I certainly want to express my deep gratitude and appreciation to my publisher, Dr. John Mabry of Apocryphile Press, for his skilled guidance and willingness to work with me, and for the work of our extremely talented editor, Dr. Janeen Jones.

And, of course, these acknowledgments would not be complete without thanking those who have served along the way as invaluable spiritual companions and friends, listening to me and sitting with me during my times of my losses and transitions as an adult: Laurie Maclean, Glenna Mahoney, Dennis Winzenried, Rev. Marshall Scott, Rev. Joe Alford, David Kell, and Jay Giulvezan.

Finally, to my spiritual director of over 20 years, Sr. Micaela Randolph, OSB, and the staff and my colleagues at the Sophia Center and Souljourners, thank you all.

About the Author

Alan has served as both a spiritual care and bereavement coordinator for hospices, hospitals, and long-term care facilities for 20 years. He earned his Master of Education in Counseling from the University of Missouri at Columbia, his Master of Business Administration from Rockhurst University, and his Doctor of Theology degree in Multifaith Spiritual Direction from the Spiritual Care Association's University of Theology and Spirituality. He has taught at the university level and has been licensed in fields as diverse as counseling, nursing, and finance. He is drawn to monasticism, not in a cloistered religious community, but as one with the heart of a monk—in the world, but not of the world. He made his profession as an Associate of the Order of Holy Cross (an order founded on the Rule of Saint Benedict) in 1999, where he has continued to serve as an Associate.

As a board-certified life coach, Alan guides and supports others professionally as a spiritual advisor and as a grief transitions coach. He especially finds meaning in working with those who have experienced losses and are struggling with grief, those in transition, and those moving into—or solidly in—their later years, and with those moving from career into retirement. As in the Japanese tradition of Kintsugi, Alan looks for new beauty in his clients' lives as they transform their broken places to new places of strength and luminescence. In this way, he has come to see people as more than whole, even if they do not see themselves that way.

The reflections and lessons of our character Rob have been drawn from many of my own experiences, both professional and personal. This book, therefore, is a blend of fiction and nonfiction; in truth, I don't think that it could have been anything else. I invite you to ride along with us for his wake-up call and retreat, benefitting from his lessons as he shares them on his journey—a journey to the discovery of the needs, values, and practices of belonging, connection, and meaning.

www.ingramcontent.com/pod-product-compliance
Lightning Source LLC
Chambersburg PA
CBHW031321160426
43196CB00007B/608